W9-DEC-067

THE

REFERENCE

SHELF

PS
668
.B3
1995-96

REPRESENTATIVE AMERICAN SPEECHES 1995-1996

Edited by CALVIN McLEOD LOGUE
Josiah Meigs Professor of Speech
University of Georgia

and

JEAN DeHART
Assistant Professor of Communication Arts
Appalachian State University

THE REFERENCE SHELF

Volume 68 Number 6

THE H. W. WILSON COMPANY

New York   Dublin   1996

GOSHEN COLLEGE LIBRARY
GOSHEN, INDIANA

THE REFERENCE SHELF

The books in this series contain reprints of articles, excerpts from books, and addresses on current issues and social trends in the United States and other countries. There are six numbers to a volume, all of which are usually published in a single calendar year. Numbers one through five devote themselves to a single subject and give background information and discussion from various points of view, concluding with a comprehensive bibliography that contains books, pamphlets, and abstracts of additional articles on the subject. The final number is a collection of recent speeches. This number also contains a subject index to the entire Reference Shelf volume. Books in the series may be purchased individually or on subscription.

Visit H. W. Wilson's web site at: http://www.hwwilson.com

Library of Congress has cataloged this serial title as follows:

Representative American speeches. 1937/38–
    New York, H. W. Wilson Co.
      v. 21 cm.--(The Reference shelf)
    Annual.
    Indexes:
      Author index: 1937/38–1959/60, with 1959/60;
      1960/61–1969/70, with 1969/70; 1970/71–1979/80,
      with 1979/80; 1980/81–1989/90, 1990.
    Editors: 1937/38–1958/59, A. C. Baird.--1959/60–1969/70, L.
    Thonssen.--1970/71–1979/80,   W.   W.   Braden.--1980/81
-1994/95, O. Peterson.--1995/96-　, C. M. Logue and J. DeHart.
    ISSN 0197-6923 Representative American speeches.
    1. Speeches, addresses, etc., American. 2. Speeches, addresses, etc.
    I. Baird, Albert Craig, 1883-1979 ed. II. Thonssen,
    Lester, 1904- ed. III. Braden, Waldo Warder, 1911-1991 ed.
    IV. Peterson, Owen, 1924- ed. V. Logue, Calvin McLeod, 1935-
    and DeHart, Jean.   eds. VI. Series.
PS668.B3   815.5082   38-27962
                                                       MARC-S
Library of Congress [8503r85]rev4

Copyright © 1996 by The H. W. Wilson Company. All rights reserved. No part of this work may be reproduced or copied in any form or by any means, including but not restricted to graphic, electronic, and mechanical—for example, photocopying, recording, taping, or information and retrieval systems—without the express written permission of the publisher, except that a reviewer may quote and a magazine or newspaper may print brief passages as part of a review written specifically for inclusion in that magazine or newspaper.

Printed in the United States of America

CONTENTS

PREFACE

Free expression is the lifeblood of democracy. Public discourse that is responsible and productive raises the quality of freedom's choices. Informed public address, debate, and narratives by citizens of diverse voices contribute vitally to society's progress. In our monitoring of pubic advocacy from March 1995 to April 1996, the approximate period covered by this volume, we cumulated folders of news reports, editorial comment, and public debate ranging over many subjects from abortions to welfare, and from many and varied points of view. This volume of *Representative American Speeches* embodies a number of those concerns. While some observers criticize the quality of public expression in America today, we should remember, as Andrew Delbanco teaches, that there can be "a fine line between the decline of civil discourse and the rise of critical energy" (*New York Times Book Review*, April 16, 1995).

Recurring in many of the speeches in this volume is the central question of what kind of nation the United States is to become? Can we get along as one people? Can we agree on ways to solve our problems? The speeches we have selected are divided into eight thematic sections: civil discourse, the nature of government, the environment, race, women's rights and achievements, media, religion, and continuing education. *Representative American Speeches* publishes only complete speeches.

The speeches in Section I call for a more civil public discourse and greater acceptance of personal responsibility. Fearful of the intolerance and violence too often experienced in America, speakers warn of dire consequences of the "language of hate" they hear in the public forum, neighborhoods, the school house, and elsewhere. For example, according to a *Times Mirror* Center study, 77% of the general public gave Washington officials a "low rating for honesty and ethics" (William Glaberson, *New York Times*, May 22, 1995). Many in public life equate political compromise with weakness or failure. Concerned about a lack of decorum in academic discourse, in 1994, professors at the Stanford Institute for Higher Education Research examined civil communication in a paper, "Hollowed Collegiality: Implications for Teaching Quality" (Courtney Leatherman, *Chronicle of Higher*

Education, March 8, 1996). To achieve a more constructive and beneficial dialogue, in Atlanta, Georgia, Kennesaw State College and the Humanities Council sponsored programs to foster "civil discourse on a range of heated topics" (editorial, *Atlanta Constitution*, Aug. 30, 1995).

The speeches in Section II debate what should be the function, size, and cost of government. While willing to downsize some agencies, President Clinton's Democratic administration strives to protect Medicare, Medicaid, education, and the environment, while on the other side, a Republican-led Congress insists on less government, lower taxes, and fewer regulations. By August 1995, a *New York Times* CBS poll found that only 26% of Americans thought either the Clinton Administration or the Republicans were serious about solving the nation's problems. By November, impatient with what many perceived to be self-indulgent bickering, 62% of respondents "favored formation of a new party" (Gallup, Everett Carll Ladd, *Chronicle of Higher Education*, Nov. 24, 1995). This "Clash of Cultures" eventually led, for a brief period, to the shut-down of all but essential departments of the federal government.

Section III contains speeches on the environment and the question of whether the nation's priority should be preserving the earth's resources or strengthening the nation's economy.

The speeches in Section IV address a complex array of issues linked to the general theme of race. With several state governments and federal courts abolishing or curtailing affirmative action initiatives, some of the speakers ask what should be done to ensure equity of opportunity for minorities.

The speeches in Section V deal with the achievements, opportunities, and rights of women.

With many Americans now blaming television primarily for the current rates of teen-age sex and violence (*New York Times* poll, Aug. 20, 1995), the speeches in Section VI explore the nature, function, and responsibility of the various media, including newspapers, entertainment, and information technology.

During 1995–1996, many Americans from all walks of life expressed the desire for a more ethical community. In Section VII, both laypersons and clerics of different religious affiliations advocate the importance of religious values for tolerance, dialogue, candor, honesty, and commitment in our public and private dealings.

The speeches in Section VIII are on various dimensions and conditions of continuing education, including solidarity, literacy, health, personal resolve, safety, and morality.

The editors are gratified to follow in the distinguished tradition of A. Craig Baird, Lester Thonssen, Waldo W. Braden, and Owen Peterson, mentors distant and near. For providing information or assistance, we express appreciation to Stephen Braden, John L. Campbell, Karlyn Kohrs Campbell, Eugene Miller, Owen Peterson, John Prechtel, Jeanette Reid, Don Rubin, Chris Schroll, Doyle Srader, Susan Tuggle, Kim Verdell, and the speakers and their staffs. We also wish to thank the General Publications staff of the H. W. Wilson Company, and the library staffs at the University of Georgia and Appalachian State University.

CALVIN M. LOGUE
JEAN DEHART

May 10, 1996

I. TOWARD A MORE CIVIL PUBLIC DISCOURSE

REMARKS AT MONTICELLO[1]
ROBERTO C. GOIZUETA

Chairman, Board of Directors, and chief executive officer, The Coca-Cola Company; born Havana, Cuba, 1931; B.S., Yale University, 1953; vice president, The Coca-Cola Company, 1966; senior vice president, 1974; executive vice president, 1975; vice chairman, 1979; president and chief operating officer, 1980; chairman and CEO, 1981; Ellis Island Medal of Honor; Service to Democracy Award, The American Assembly; Equal Justice Award, NAACP Legal Defense Fund.

Editors' introduction: On the Fourth of July, 1995, Mr. Roberto C. Goizueta spoke to 67 new Americans gathered at Monticello, moments before their swearing in as naturalized citizens by U.S. District Judge Jackson L. Kiser. Among some 1,500 guests assembled for the 33rd annual Independence Day Celebration and Naturalization Ceremony were family and friends of the new citizens, political and civic leaders, and representatives from the University of Virginia.

Following his address, the first by a corporate representative in the event's history, Mr. Goizueta restated his own oath of citizenship as the 67 new citizens—hailing from nations such as China, Ghana, Jordan, Korea, Russia, the United Kingdom, and Uruguay—took theirs.

The naturalization ceremony is an annual highlight of Independence Day observances at Jefferson's historic home. And for Mr. Goizueta, it was a reminder of the hot Atlanta day 26 years earlier when he became a naturalized citizen, "eyes focused on a solitary flag as I pledged allegiance to my new country."

The day's ceremonies had a patriotic flair, with the participation of the Charlottesville Municipal Band, the Monticello Color Guard, Boy Scouts, and Girl Scouts. The League of Women Voters and the Albemarle County Registrar offered voter registra-

[1]Delivered at Monticello on July 4, 1995.

tion services, and local chapters of the Sons of the American Revolution and Daughters of the American Revolution marked the event with ceremonies at President Jefferson's grave site.

Mr. Goizueta began his career with The Coca-Cola Company as a chemist in his native Havana in 1954. He left Cuba with his family in 1961, taking with him little but his education and a job with the Company—of which he was named CEO in 1981. It is from that perspective that he delivered his message of opportunity and obligation to America's newest citizens on the West Lawn at Monticello.

Mr. Roberto C. Goizueta's speech: Standing before you today—here in this hallowed place—I feel compelled to quote Thomas Jefferson himself who said, "Speeches measured by the hour . . . die by the hour."

I am also reminded of my wife's frequent observation that no one ever comes away from listening to a speech saying, "That was great . . . but I wish it had been longer."

So, in acknowledgment of the wisdom of Mr. Jefferson, . . . as well as the insightfulness of Mrs. Goizueta, . . . my message to you will be brief and to the point.

I must start by recognizing the *vision* and *determination* of those of you who are to be naturalized today as citizens of this great country.

For me, looking into your eyes this morning is like looking into a mirror . . . a mirror that takes me back 26 years . . . back to a hot, muggy day in 1969 at the Federal Building in Atlanta, Georgia.

And in that mirror of *your* eyes, I see my *own* eyes . . .

. . . eyes focused on a solitary flag as I pledged allegiance to my new country . . .

. . . eyes wide with an immeasurable sense of anticipation, excitement and opportunity . . .

. . . eyes brightened by a deep sense of gratitude . . .

. . . and, yes, eyes determined to remain dry despite the sobering knowledge of the tragic fate being forced on the Cuban people by a communist regime.

It is your *vision* of a better life that has brought you to this place today. And it is your *decisiveness* . . . as the masters of your own destiny . . . that has made this moment a reality.

I congratulate you on this accomplishment. I salute you for your resolve. And I am indebted to you for providing me with this vivid reminder of one of the most significant days in my own history.

Together, we share a truly magical gift . . . the magical gift of freedom . . . and with it, its corollary we refer to as "opportunity."

When my family and I came to this country . . . we had to leave everything behind. Back in Havana, our family photographs hung on the walls. Our wedding gifts sat on the shelves. Every material property we owned, . . . overnight became government property.

But amid that turmoil, two treasured possessions remained mine because they simply could not be taken away by the newly arrived Cuban rulers.

Firstly, even though I had to leave behind my diploma from Yale . . .

. . . and even though I had to leave behind the Webster's dictionary I earned as valedictorian of my high school graduating class, . . . I carried with me, . . . safely in my head, . . . the meaning of that diploma and of that dictionary.

. . . I still had my education.

And secondly, even though the Havana Coca-Cola bottling plant where I had worked was to be confiscated,

. . . I still had a job.

And it wasn't just any job. It was a job with The Coca-Cola Company.

From that point on—as you might guess—the story improves significantly.

And that story—*my* story—boils down to a single, inspiring reality

. . . the reality that a young immigrant could come to this country . . . be given a chance to work hard and apply his skills . . . and ultimately earn the opportunity to lead not only a large corporation . . .

. . . but an institution that actually symbolizes the very essence of America and American ideals.

Not a bad story . . .

. . . but, what has it taught me?

Let me tell you—it has taught me a great deal. But first and foremost, it has taught me that *opportunity* always comes accompanied by *obligations*.

And, what are the obligations which come with opportunity?, (you may ask.)

Each of us, of course, must answer that question on our own. But in my life, I have found that every opportunity I have ever encountered has implied three fundamental obligations.

The first obligation implied in opportunity is that you must *seize* it. You must reach out to the opportunity . . . take it in your hands . . . and mold it into a work that brings value to your society.

To do otherwise, is not just a waste . . . it is a crime against the human spirit. Squandering what the rest of the world covets is not only foolish . . . it is immoral.

The second obligation which naturally follows opportunity is that you must *live* it . . . you must carry it on your back all day long . . . you must sense the opportunity in your nostrils with every breath . . .

. . . and you must see it in your dreams when you are asleep.

Because even though opportunity—much like freedom itself—is born only out of ideals, . . . it is nurtured only by action . . .

Without action . . . opportunity and freedom soon shrivel and fade to a slow death.

Finally, the third obligation which inherently comes with opportunity is that you must *defend* it.

Thomas Jefferson said, "The tree of liberty must be refreshed from time to time with the blood of patriots and tyrants."

And, yes—*from time to time*—that is unfortunately true . . . painfully true.

But the tree of liberty must also be irrigated—irrigated *every single day*—with the sweat off the brows of enterprising men and women, . . .

. . . men and women working hard to further prove the inherent superiority of a democratic society, . . .

. . . working hard to demonstrate the lasting stability of a democratic capitalistic system, . . .

. . . working hard to preserve the sanctity of private property, . . .

. . . working hard to continue to show the world that people *can* indeed be trusted with governing themselves, . . .

. . . , as the man who built this house said, men and women working hard to put the interests of our nation ahead of their own personal interests.

To my mind, those are the three obligations we owe opportunity.

They are simple.

They are undeniable.

They are demanding.

And, most of all, they are yours and mine to embrace . . . or to reject.

Opportunity . . .

. . . ours to seize . . .

. . . ours to live . . .

. . . and ours to defend.

Or otherwise—ultimately—ours to lose.

Like many of you here today, I know what it's like to lose what had taken many years to build. And just like you, I refuse to suffer through that kind of loss ever again.

And so, I challenge you and every other citizen across our nation—whether native-born or naturalized—to embrace your individual obligations . . . to embrace your individual obligations as if the fate of the United States depended on it.

And you know why? . . . because—in reality—it does.

I thank you, and the trustees of the Thomas Jefferson Memorial Foundation, for giving me this opportunity today. And I wish each of you new Americans the fullest blessings that come with true freedom and opportunity.

PARTICIPATING IN THE PROCESS[2]
JANET RENO

United States Attorney General; born Miami, FL, 1938; A.B., Cornell University, 1938; LL.B., Harvard University, 1963; Steel, Hector &

[2]Delivered at the Santa Clara University Law School, CA, on May 20, 1995.

Davis law firm, Miami, FL, 1976–78; State Attorney for Dade County, FL, 1978–93; Herbert Harley Award, American Judicature Society, 1981; Medal of Honor, Florida Bar Association, 1990.

Editors' introduction: On April 19, 1995, a bombing at the Alfred P. Murrah federal building in Oklahoma City killed and wounded men, women, and children. Reaction to the bombing was one of great anger and pain over loss of human life, and a renewed determination to stop terrorists. President Clinton directed Attorney General Janet Reno to check security conditions at all Federal buildings, and called for expanded federal powers with which to monitor suspected terrorists. Upon the advice of the Secret Service, Clinton had concrete barriers erected on Pennsylvania Avenue in front of the White House. Some demanded closer monitoring of various militia groups active throughout the United States. At the same time, the *New York Times* (April 21, 1995) editorial and the American Civil Liberties Union (Todd S. Purdum, *New York Times*, April 24, 1995) cautioned officials not to overreact. In a speech at Michigan State University, on May 5, 1995, Clinton spoke of "dark possibilities of our age . . . visible now in the smoke, the horror, and the heartbreak of Oklahoma . . . with 165 dead, 467 injured, and two still unaccounted for." He commended militia members who "condemn[ed] the bombing," and warned others they had no right to resort to violence.

Within this violent climate, on May 20, 1995, Attorney General Reno spoke to the Santa Clara University Law School graduation audience in California. The morning ceremony took place outdoors in the campus' historic mission gardens, with about 3,000 alumni, family members, and reporters expected. The *San Francisco Chronicle* (Maria Alicia Gaura, May 20, 1995) reported that due to the Oklahoma City bombing, even greater precautions were taken and her appearance was kept secret for a couple of months. Gaura stated that, "the nation's first woman attorney general, Reno has won praise and support for her plain-spoken ways and her willingness to take responsibility for blunders by her department." Reno, empathizing with citizens racked by a terrible violence, sought to heal their wounds.

Janet Reno's speech: Thank you Father, thank you Dean Player, and, to the graduates, to the faculty, to the family and friends who helped the graduates get here, thank you for this high honor, for this degree from a great law school and a great university.

From this law school, from this great land of the west with its rich and wonderfully old heritage, but a land that is also taking us into the twenty-first century, from the family and friends that surround you today, you will draw strength and courage and wisdom for the rest of your life.

It has been a little over two years ago that I came to Washington to face one of the greatest challenges that any lawyer could undertake. I came alon[e] but, in so many respects, I was not alone. Memories and spirit and people came with me; their spirit was with me. My law school dean was with me, the man who admitted women to Harvard Law School and encouraged us to continue our efforts, a man who over these 30 years until he died last year made it a point of seeking me out at bar meetings to keep me encouraged and supported every step of the way.

It was my American history teacher in high school who got me to thinking that I really could be a lawyer; it was my college roommate who gave me coffee at 2:00 a.m. in the morning as I was trying to prepare for my Constitutional Law course; it was the brother who teased me unmercifully as I was growing up, and even to this day calls me to tease me when he thinks I'm getting too big headed; there was my baby sitter who called from all the way across the nation to tell me how proud he was of me.

All of these people, and so many more, have been with me every step of the way. And the lessons that I have learned along the way have been with me.

The Dean made reference to a house. When I came to Washington, I suddenly found—and I guess I knew it but it hits you with a grim reality that you're responsible for the FBI, the DEA, the Bureau of Prisons, Immigration and Naturalization, and most of the government's lawyers—and you say, where do I begin?

I was reminded of the afternoon my mother picked us up at school. We had lived in a small, little wooden house that was too big for the children who were growing fast. My father didn't have enough money to hire a contractor to build the house and my mother announced that she was going to build the house. And we said, "What do you know about building a house?" She said, "I'm going to learn."

And she went to the brick mason, to the electrician, to the plumber and she talked to them about how to build a house; and she built the house. She dug the foundation with a pick and shovel, she laid the block, she put in the wiring and the plumbing; and my father would help her with the heavy beams when he came home from work at night.

She and I lived in that house till just before she died, before I came to Washington when she died. And every time I came down the driveway and saw that house standing there, as a prosecutor, as a lawyer having a difficult problem to solve, that house was a symbol to me that you can do anything you really want to if it's the right thing to do and you put your mind to it.

But that house taught me a more important lesson on August the 24th, 1992, when hurricane Andrew hit the area and devastated it. About 3:00 in the morning, my mother got up as the winds began to howl. She was old and frail and dying, but she was totally unafraid. She went over and sat down in her chair, folded her hands and, as the winds crashed trees around the house, she just sat there, for she knew how she had built that house; she had not cut corners, she put in good materials, she'd done it the right way.

When we came out in the early dawn, it looked like a World War I battlefield, but the house had only lost one shingle and some screens. That's the lesson that I carried with me to Washington in trying to figure out how to begin to administer the Department of Justice.

And so, draw strength and understanding and wisdom from those who have touched your lives, from the lessons that you've learned and will learn along the way, and go forth to use the law, its principles and its processes, to help others. Go forth and be yourself. Be known for who you are, not for the law firm you're with, not for the house that you live in, not for the money you make, but be known for who you are, what you stand for, and what you do for others.

The law has been a marvelous instrument for me; I have loved it, I have loved what it can do for people. And there are challenges that all of us, the new graduates, the Attorney General, the seasoned practitioner, all of us face. First, we have watched this nation racked by a terrible violence in this past month but we saw this nation come together in a remarkable way. We saw the people of this nation speak out against the hatred and the violence that had spawned that blast. We saw the people of America reach out and hold the victims and the survivors and help them begin to heal.

Yesterday, I was in Oklahoma City and talked to survivors, talked to people who had been injured, talked to people who had lost loved ones, and they said the feeling that had come from across America is something that kept them going.

I have watched America reach out and support law enforcement in every step of the way in holding the people accountable for this terrible evil, in cooperating in every way possible. I have seen America speak out to ensure that we protect the freedoms and the rights that we hold so dear and that we honor the rule of law as we bring these people to justice. I have seen America reach out and defend this nation.

We criticize government, but there is no other government in the history of the world that has ever afforded its people such freedoms and such opportunities. We must continue to speak out against the hatred and the violence that would undermine it.

Lawyers sometimes tend to get stuck in their little rut, they focus just on their case, their billable hours, their clients, and they don't look beyond. And too many professions are as focused. Look beyond and remember what we stand for. We must, as a nation, continue to speak out against violence, against hatred. And there's nobody more persuasive than a good lawyer; let us put those skills to work.

You can do it in simple and small ways. For example, in Billings, Montana in November of 1993, bricks were thrown into the homes of two Jewish families in the community. The *Billings Gazette* responded immediately by publishing a full-page menorah. The non-Jewish community throughout Billings started putting the menorah up in their windows; thousands of windows appeared with menorahs. As the Jewish community worshipped at the Hanukkah service, non-Jewish people stood outside to make sure that nothing happened and those responsible faded away.

We have seen another example this past week of a profile of someone speaking out. We're not Republicans and Democrats in this process, we're Americans as we speak out. And I applaud George Bush for his actions and for his eloquence when he resigned his membership with the NRA. It is a true test of leadership when you're able to tell your friends they're wrong. Demonizing the men and women of law enforcement who put their lives on the line each day in defense of our freedoms is just plain wrong.

Everyone in public life, every lawyer, every American, can learn from the powerful example of President Bush that there are times when you have to tell your friends they've done the wrong thing.

And we must think in other contexts. I will always remember my father who came as a twelve-year-old to Racine, Wisconsin. He spoke not a word of English. He never forgot that people teased him about his funny language and his funny clothes and he tried to be kind to people for the rest of his life. Four years later, he was the editor of a high school newspaper; and, for 43 years, he wrote beautiful English for the *Miami Herald*.

We must remember where we came from and speak out against bigotry, speak out against those who would be intolerant.

Secondly, get involved, don't sit on the sidelines; use the remarkable skills that you've developed here either as a negotiator, litigator, or just a person who thinks with the common sense and applies it to the law.

Public service is a wonderful opportunity. When I graduated from Harvard Law School in 1963 and couldn't get the job that I wanted, I was envious of those lawyers going on to Wall Street and to silk-stocking firms across the country. Now, as I meet them, they are envious of my opportunity and my career for public service.

You don't have to do just one or the other; but public service along the way is an experience and an opportunity that you will never forget.

Think broadly. I swore I would never be a prosecutor; I thought prosecutors were more interested in securing convictions than seeking justice. My predecessor suggested that I might become the State Attorney and do something about that concept. But, if you become a prosecutor, think beyond. This is a great nation but it's a nation that can be improved on; and let's work to do it.

The prosecutor who convicts that person and sends him to jail and doesn't make sure that we have enough jail cells, doesn't make sure we have good treatment in the jails to solve the problem that caused him to go there in the first place, is not the prosecutor doing his or her job.

Public defenders are so important. It is something I will never forget: about ten years ago, a young man came up to me and said, "You defended me when I was a juvenile. I was charged with a delinquent act. You got me off on the right foot. And I'm married, I've got a job; everything's been okay ever since."

But the prosecutor or the public defender who ends the job in the court room isn't doing the job. That public defender who watches somebody walk out the court room free on a motion to dismiss, knowing they have a crack addiction, who doesn't try to do something about it, either in changing attitudes in the legislature, changing attitudes in Congress or trying to find a treatment program that will provide that help, isn't doing his or her best to help the client.

But, if you don't want public service, just think about what you can do as a lawyer participating in the process. Too many lawyers get into it from a narrow self-interest. Somebody is trying to rezone property next to them, they get upset with city hall, they get into the zoning battle, they learn about it, and some of them just turn away after they've won their battle and go back to what they were doing. But more and more and more, lawyers are getting involved in the processes of government as lay people working from the outside to improve government and to make it more real for all people. Don't sit on the sidelines.

I invite all of you to come to the Department of Justice one day, to the Attorney General's conference room, and look at the two great murals that were put on those walls in 1937. One is a mural of justice granted, a hopeful scene of people progressing with great industry, with art and music, towards a better future; the other is justice denied, a wasteland of brown-shirted thugs taking people out in chains to prisons, of brown-shirted thugs breaking violins and taking pens and paper. Those murals were put on the wall of the Department of Justice in 1937, four years before we went into World War II, four years before we really spoke out against tyranny. We cannot sit on the sidelines.

And, in one area, all of us must focus attention; we have sat on the sidelines, been indifferent, and ignored the future of America for too long. Our children are our most precious possession; but our children are being killed on the streets of America, our children are not getting the education they need, our children are not getting the development and the opportunity and the positive structure they need to grow to be strong, constructive human beings. And too many lawyers along the way have focused on a personal injury law suit or a large corporate transaction and forgotten what our future is all about.

Unless we invest in our children today and legal principles and process and structure that can give them a strong and positive future, we are not going to have a work force with the skills that can fill the jobs that can maintain this nation as a first-rate nation.

I love lawyers because they can be so creative, so innovative, so bold; let us take the creativity, the energy, the intellect that abounds across the campuses of the great universities of this nation here today and put it to work as an investment in our future, not in smokestacks, not in technology, but in what counts most, our people. And to do that, we have to concentrate on a third issue; we've got to make the law real for all Americans.

The American Bar Association has done a study in which they found that about half of those households of 3,000 low- and moderate-income households have at least one legal need. The most prominent was for personal finances, consumer issues, housing and real property, personal and economic injury, wills and estates, and family law. The sad conclusion of that survey is that 71 percent of low-income and 61 percent of moderate-income legal needs are not being addressed by the civil justice system in America today. What that means is that, for far too many Americans, the law is worth little more than the paper it's written on.

Too many Americans feel disenfranchised and that they can't get their problems solved. Too many Americans have confronted lawyers who get them a judgment then don't follow through. Too many Americans have gotten lawyers who don't listen to them and are more interested in the processes of the court that don't go to solving the person's problem.

On the east wall of the building of the Department of Justice in Washington is a statement chiseled into the stone. It says, "The common law is derived from the will of mankind issuing from the people, framed by mutual confidence, and sanctioned by the light of reason." If people do not have access to the law, if they do not feel part of the law, they become disenfranchised and opposed. All of us, as lawyers, have a special responsibility to make the law real for all Americans.

We can begin to start speaking in small, old words and get rid of, once and for all, the legalese that has dominated this profession for too long. We can start speaking in terms that people can understand rather than Roman numerals and alphabets and titles that they don't understand. We can go to legislatures, we can go to court processes and rules and start framing issues in ways that people can understand. The average person is real smart until lawyers start confusing the issues sometimes.

But most of all, we have got to remember that the law is people. It is not a motion to dismiss, it is not a Federal Rule of Civil Procedure, it is not a judgment that is the goal. What we are trying to do is solve people's problems and protect their freedoms and protect their interests. And, to solve people's problems, we have to listen to them and look at them as if they are the most important people around, not as if we're trying to see our next appointment or are more interested in our billable hours. We have got to figure out how to solve people's problems.

Some are concerned about lawyer-bashing in this country; I think the greatest single thing we can do about that attitude is to solve people's problems, do it in a cost-effective way, do it in a caring way, and make a difference.

But the most important thing I urge you to consider as you start this great adventure is remember the most precious possession you have and will have, your family and your friends.

I remember that lady who built the house. She worked in the home when she wasn't building the house; she taught us to play baseball, to bake sponge cakes, to appreciate Beethoven's symphonies. She taught us her favorite poets, she taught us to play fair, she loved us with all her heart. And there is no childcare in the world that will ever be a substitute for what that lady was in our life.

I look at the young lawyers in America today trying to raise families; getting breakfast on the table and the children off to school; coming home after trial after they've prepped their witnesses for the next day; getting through the last vestiges of rush hour; putting dinner on the table; getting the children bathed, their homework done. Saturdays, they run errands; Sundays, they start preparing for trial again. And suddenly, the six-year-olds will be 16 and 26 before they know it.

Bringing up a child is the single most difficult thing I have ever done in my life. A little over ten years ago a friend died leaving me as the legal guardian for her 15-year-old twins, a boy and a girl. The girl was in love; and I've learned an awful lot about raising children in the last ten years.

I've learned it takes intelligence, hard work, luck, and an awful lot of love; but I have also learned that it is one of the most rewarding experiences that you can have, to send a young lady off to college and then see her graduate cum laude in three years and, on those occasions, have her throw her arms around my neck and say, "Thank you, I couldn't have done it without you."

All I ask of you as you go out in this wonderful new career is remember your family, remember the children that you will have. If we can send a man to the moon, surely, surely, surely; we can achieve professional fulfillment while at the same time putting our children and our family first.

When you go to that law firm, when you go to that Department of Justice, the public defender's office, the prosecutor's office, ask them about flex time and telecommuting for both parents, not just for one.

And then, as you remember all the people that have touched your life, as you remember this place, go forth, build a strong family, develop a practice that helps others truly, and go out and let us find peace in this world.

God bless you all.

THE ESSENCE OF FREE SPEECH[3]
RICHARD D. HEFFNER

University Professor of Communications and Public Policy, Rutgers University; born New York City, 1925; A.B., 1946 and M.A., 1947, Columbia University; Producer and Moderator of "The Open Mind," public television, New York City; Chair of the Board and Administrator of the motion picture industry's voluntary film classification system, 1974–94; consultant; editor; author.

Editors' introduction: Following the bombing of a Federal building in Oklahoma City, in a speech to the American Association of Community Colleges in Minneapolis, President Clinton criticized those who spread hate in America, remarking, "when they talk of hatred, we must stand against them." In editorials, while supporting freedom of speech, the *New York Times* (April 25 & 27, 1995) warned that "virulent speakers who characterize

[3]Delivered at Rutgers University, New Brunswick, NJ, on May 18, 1995, at 2 p.m.

politics as warfare and opponents as demon[s] can create an environment in which violence blossoms."

To awaken his audience to the danger of hate speech, on May 18, 1995, Professor Richard D. Heffner spoke from a prepared manuscript to 2,000 graduates, their families, and friends convened at Rutgers University's 229th commencement. Seniors honored by their respective academic departments also spoke. Heffner explained to the editors of this volume that his strategy was to "quote . . . authorities about past loss of faith in reason." "I believe both students and faculty," Heffner recalled, "were initially dismayed by my seeming concern that unlimited free speech may have its own limitations, and by my suggestion that reason in our age is endangered." An excerpt of Heffner's speech was published in the *Chronicle of Higher Education* (June 9, 1995).

Richard D. Heffner's speech: Graduates, Colleagues, Friends . . .

Being here today is both an honor and a welcome spur to warm and good memories of first coming to Rutgers College nearly half a century ago . . . as a young Instructor then in American History and Political Science. My first full-time teaching appointment . . . and an enormously heady and intellectually challenging work experience.

Indeed, it was the most exciting and hopeful possible time to be involved in the Academy, to be involved with the life of the mind, the life of reason . . . to which as friend *and* teacher to many of you today I truly hope you will repair in some way, to some important degree . . . *whatever* work or career choices you make.

Many of my students then were older than I was: mature, purposeful, self-disciplined, intellectually demanding of themselves . . . and of their faculty. They were mostly World War II veterans, here at Rutgers thanks to the G.I. Bill, that best possible symbol of a wisely activist and generous nation's gratitude for service in the war against totalitarianism just ended.

A symbol, too, of this nation's profound understanding (in *those* years, if not in *these*) that our future well-being could best be entrusted to educated men and women who would take from the faith in them thus demonstrated, and from the enormous resources so generously committed to them, the firm belief that America's future could and would be bright . . . that literally with the shooting and the shouting over, trained reason could and would now prevail, bringing with it the Good Life, one of peace and plenty and progress.

Yes, it was a wonderfully hopeful time . . . one filled with an abiding faith in human reason, in mankind's essential capacity for rationality, for open mindedness, for that fair and balanced and civilized discourse that must undergird any democratic society if it is to prevail.

Then our faith was John Milton's: "Whoever knew truth put to the worse in a free and open encounter."

How different, of course, from the grim war-time warnings set forth just a half decade before by philosophers John Dewey, Sidney Hook, and Ernest Nagel in their memorable 1943 *Partisan Review* Symposium on "The New Failure of Nerve."

Hook had reminded us that in the famous third chapter of his *Four Stages of Greek Religion*, scholar and critic Gilbert Murray had characterized the period from 300 B.C. through the first century of the Christian era as marked by a "failure of nerve," one exhibited in "a rise of asceticism, of mysticism, in a sense, of pessimism; a loss of self-confidence, of hope in *this* life and of faith in *normal* human efforts; a departure from patient inquiry, a cry for infallible revelation: an indifference to the welfare of the state. . . . "

Then Hook wrote that a survey of the cultural tendencies of his own time showed "many signs pointing to *a new failure of nerve* in Western civilization . . . more complex and sophisticated than in any previous time . . . it betrays . . . the same flight from responsibility . . . that drove the ancient world into the shelters of . . . supernaturalism."

"There is hardly a field," Hook insisted, "from which these signs of intellectual panic, heralded as portents of spiritual revival, are lacking . . . the recrudescence of beliefs in the original depravity of human nature; prophecies of doom for Western culture dressed up as laws of social dynamics; the frenzied search for a center of value that transcends human interests . . . *contempt for all political organizations and social programs because of the obvious failure of some of them* . . . the refurbishing of theological and metaphysical dogmas abut the infinite as necessary presuppositions of knowledge of the finite." Thus, he concluded, "*Obscurantism is no longer apologetic*; it has now become precious and willful."

Yet by 1948, when I came here to teach, that obscurantism had happily been defeated, even as V-E Day and then V-J Day had marked the defeat of the Axis Powers themselves. Human reason again seemed triumphant; no failure of nerve on the campus then, or in our country generally . . . but rather an abiding faith, if you will, in mankind's infinite capacity to deal thoughtfully, reasonably and well with whatever problems an educated, measured, and fair-minded people might face.

But a faith that now must *once again* be rekindled and defended! And *you* must be its instrument . . . though facing threats perhaps as great as those that challenged depression—and then wartime—America, in the 1930's and early 40's.

For there are signs in our times, distressing signs, that many Americans are *once again* experiencing that "failure of nerve" in a reasoned and reasoning way of life, a failure your generation can ill afford and must combat at all costs.

More than ever before, your generation must reject those who counsel despair and intellectual panic, who no longer find democracy serviceable or our political and governmental institutions competent to serve our national and our individual needs.

Yes, these are stressful times—particularly as we move from one century to the next—but times made much more so by the paranoid insistence that America's political and governmental institutions are not *ours* any longer, but rather *others'* . . . that the laws and leaders of this generation no longer reflect *our* interests, but rather *others*, that they can and must therefore be defamed and defied . . . indeed, with impunity.

Yet you young Americans *needn't* now fail our history *and* our heritage. You needn't make nor permit others to make such fair game of our public institutions and leadership by tolerating, thus indeed by exacerbating, an increasingly irrational and vicious disdain and contempt for *all* political organizations and social programs because of the obvious inadequacies of *some* of them.

Too many Americans have been carried away by the gross misrepresentations of those who would manipulate and engineer our consent to their paranoid assumption that *others*—African Americans, Jews, Environmentalists, Hispanics, Feminists, Asian Americans, the United Nations—*others*, always *others*, would do us in, their paranoid assumption that our own government day and night musters its forces in a grave conspiracy to deprive us of our freedoms.

But you needn't, mustn't, embrace nor nurture that irratio-
nality becoming epidemic today, that failure of nerve nowhere
more viciously expressed than in the unreasoning fear of our de-
mocratically chosen leaders, and in the snarling, raging words
that accompany that fear, words that would make of mindless but
naive and misinformed malcontents accessories to mayhem and
even murder.

Indeed, I believe that the harshest challenge to face this graduating class today relates to words, to speech that is at once unreasoning, irresponsible, but that—at least within the past
parameters of the American experience—has largely been irre-
pressible. It relates to the language of hate, of fear, of violence . . . whether on the campus, on talk radio, in pseudo-
pulpits, in primers on how-to-build-a-bomb, in pernicious Willie
Horton-like political advertising, or—as entertainment or information for profit — on television, cable, home videos or games,
your personal computers, the silver screen, the information superhighway, or what-have-you.

That is going to be *your* task, you of the Class of '95, the task
of reconciling what Americans have simply not *had* to reconcile
before: the needs and purposes of what our Founders *meant* by
free speech with the needs and purposes of that domestic tran-
quility and general welfare *in whose service* they wrote both the
Constitution and its Bill of Rights.

To be sure, of our contemporaries who remain free speech
absolutists (*I* prefer for them that other wonderfully evocative de-
scriptive: "free speech voluptuaries" . . . for I think that at this
juncture in world history they *do* now largely indulge themselves),
many will consider that what I set before you today are "fighting
words"—"words that wound."

For the questions raised by the very language of violence and
hate, and in turn by what we must at least *consider* to be appropri-
ate regulatory responses *in our times* (*not* retrospectively, in older,
better, individualistic times, but in *our* increasingly interdependent and ever more parlous times), these questions occasioned by
the language of violence and hate undeniably *do* present a clear
and present danger to values thoughtful Americans have so
warmly embraced for all the earlier days of our years . . . values
that in our *past* have, indeed, marked the very genius of our national experience. But values, I submit, that *do* not, *could* not, *today*
sustain the same scrutiny and burden of interpretation appropri-
ate two centuries ago.

Perhaps Floyd Abrams, my dear friend and America's most astute Constitutional attorney, put it best . . . surely most simply and directly, as is his wont: "Americans made a brave and sophisticated choice" he has said, in deciding to endure *hateful* speech in the interest of the greater good of free and robust *political* speech.

As the popular American lyric put it: "You can't have one without the other." *Hateful* speech, then, was the price we paid for robust *political* speech. But *can* we actually *afford* any longer to carry that tune, still sing that song?

Many of us, albeit with difficulty, have come to think not. For the very choice that in Floyd Abrams' words was "brave and sophisticated" in the 18th century, may be unwise and unwarranted in the 21st.

It was about slavery and the possibility, ultimately, of emancipation that Abraham Lincoln wrote, "I shall adopt new views so fast as they shall appear to be true views." And he did. Are *we*, however, to be *less* aware that even ancient verities often must be honored in their newer, their truer, settings . . . from newer and truer perspectives?

In a very different area of concern, but one equally pressing, surely the enormous power of modern nuclear weaponry has forced the wiser among us to view *sovereignty* differently than we had earlier . . . to insist upon limiting in *these* times national military power that in *those* times was not to be limited, to respect the overwhelming nature of military might in our own times by imposing upon nations' once unbridled sovereignty and self-determination restraints *now* that were considered anathema *then*. Newer views have appeared to be truer views, and we have adopted them. Is mankind not safer as a consequence?

Similarly, have not the power of the word and the power of the picture, too, grown enormously—and dangerously—as well? And mustn't attention be paid, too, to *their* real role in our lives *today* . . . when *their* potential for posing instant and overwhelming, clear and present danger to us, to all mankind, is ever greater, too?

If within the context of near 21st century realities we do now manage essentially to *preserve* sovereignty by wisely and purposefully establishing its parameters, mustn't we similarly preserve the *essence* of free speech by as wisely and as purposefully recognizing and regulating *its* necessary new parameters?

If the words and pictures of violence and hate do now endanger us in this ever smaller space we occupy, mustn't we choose them ever more carefully and responsibly, regulating them when wisdom dictates?

Could it possibly be otherwise than that we no longer can *afford* the unquestioned and voluptuous pleasures of absolute, untrammeled speech, even as the language and pictures of violence and hate provoke, often invite, the hateful *deeds* that so often follow hateful *words*, even as such words themselves *become* such deeds.

Not *always* is it so, to be sure, perhaps only seldom, but intolerably more and more so in a time of ever greater psychological as well as physical proximity and interdependence. And a rational people can—must!—make that distinction. Indeed, that must be *your* article of faith.

We may not *want* to live on a smaller planet in which much, much more than just metaphorically the hipbone is so clearly connected to the thighbone . . . and what we say and do every day and in every way so clearly and forcefully impacts upon our neighbors that we must be as concerned for their interests and well being as for our own. But in fact we *must* now choose our *words* and our *pictures* as carefully as we would our *deeds*. Because today, in *your* time as never before, words and pictures *do* have the power to *wound* as readily as to *bind up* a nation's wounds.

In "Paradise Lost," John Milton wrote that "Good, the more communicated, more abundant grows." Can we doubt that Evil, too, "the more communicated, more abundant grows?" In our times it is *not* in order to be considered "politically correct," but simply to survive with more rather than less of our historic sense of what it takes to nourish the Good Society still intact, that now we must so much more critically evaluate the counsel of speech absolutism and recognize more effectively the clear and present danger posed by the language and imagery of violence and hate.

Yes, "Who ever knew truth put to the worse in a free and open encounter?" But the language of violence and hate does not nurture free and open encounters. It destroys them. And you of the Class of 1995 must neither foolishly nor innocently permit yourselves or your most basic values to be destroyed in the indulgent embrace of speech absolutism. As new views *do* appear to be true views . . . you, too, must adopt them.

Thank you . . . and good luck.

CIVILITY IN THE UNITED STATES SENATE[4]
Robert C. Byrd

United States Senator, 1959– ; born 1917, North Wilkesboro, NC; orphaned and brought to West Virginia; welder on World War II ships; B.A., Marshall University; LL.B, American University, 1963; Senate Majority Leader, 1977–80, 1987–88; Senate Minority Leader, 1981–86; author of Addresses on the History of the United States Senate.

Editors' introduction: In 1994, campaigning on a new "Contract With America" for less expensive and intrusive government, Republicans gained new majorities in both the House of Representatives and the United States Senate. Later, as Republicans passed some of their promised legislation, and President Clinton vetoed other initiatives, political tempers flared. On December 20, 1995, on the floor of the United States Senate, Senator Robert C. Byrd "call[ed] attention to the general tone of incivility in the Senate and in public life" (*Congressional Record*). In addition to those viewing Byrd's speech by television over C-Span, approximately 50 members, officers, and staff of the United States Senate, and print reporters were present. Because of the importance he placed upon word choice in the speech, Byrd read from a prepared manuscript. He told the editors of this volume that response to his speech ranged "from praise to very harsh criticism, some so harsh that it was surprising." His speech "prompted . . . an apology from one Senator, and criticism from another."

Several Senators reacted to Byrd's speech in Senate debate. Thomas A. Daschle praised Byrd that his "speech ought to be reprinted and sent to every civics class in the country. . . . It ought to be studied. It ought to be respected." While admiring Senator Byrd' s knowledge of the "history, record, and decorum" of the Senate, Trent Lott, Republican, reminded listeners that debates in 1995 had been "tough . . . because . . . we are dealing with . . . fundamental changes." Lott insisted, however, that we do not have to refer to one another as "tawdry and sleazy." An-

[4]Delivered at the United States Senate, Washington, DC, on December 20, 1995.

swering Lott's criticism, Byrd recalled that he had a purpose in using those terms: "I was talking about an agreement that had been broken, not about the personality of the majority leader in that instance." Concerned about the increasing "strident tone and disrespect[ful]" language used by some, and drawing wisdom from the Bible, Byrd asked that all "rein in our tongues and lower our voices."

Robert C. Byrd's speech: Mr. President, I speak from prepared remarks because I wanted to be most careful in how I chose my words and so that I might speak as the Apostle Paul in his epistle to the Colossians admonished us to do:

Let your speech be always with grace, seasoned with salt, that ye may know how ye ought to answer every man.

Mr. President, I rise today to express my deep concern at the growing incivility in this Chamber. It reached a peak of excess on last Friday during floor debate with respect to the budget negotiations and the Continuing Resolution. One Republican Senator said that he agreed with the Minority Leader that we do have legitimate differences. "But you do not have the guts to put those legitimate differences on the table," that Senator said. He went on to state, "and then you have the gall to come to us and tell us that we ought to put another proposal on the table." Now, Mr. President, I can only presume that the Senator was directing his remarks to the Minority Leader, although he was probably including all members on this side of the aisle. He also said that the President of the United States "has, once again, proven that his commitment to principle is non-existent. He gave his word; he broke his word. It is a habit he does not seem able to break."

Mr. President, I do not know what the matter of "guts" has to do with the Continuing Resolution or budget negotiations. Simply put, those words are fighting words when used off the Senate floor. One might expect to hear them in an alehouse or beer tavern, where the response would likely be the breaking of a bottle over the ear of the one uttering the provocation, or in a pool hall, where the results might be the cracking of a cue stick on the skull of the provocator. Do we have to resort to such language in this forum? In the past century, such words would be responded to by an invitation to a duel.

And who is to judge another person's commitment to principle as being nonexistent?

I am not in a position to judge that with respect to any other man or woman in this Chamber or on this Earth.

Mr. President, the Senator who made these statements is one whom I have known to be amiable and reasonable. I like him. And I was shocked to hear such strident words used by him, with such a strident tone. I hope that we will all exercise a greater restraint upon our passions and avoid making extreme statements that can only serve to further polarize the relationships between the two parties in this Chamber and between the executive and legislative branches. By all means, we should dampen our impulses to engage in personal invective.

Another Senator, who is very new around here, made the statement—and I quote from last Friday's RECORD: "This President just does not know how to tell the truth anymore," and then accused the President of stating to "the American public—bald-faced untruths." The Senator went on to say that, "we are tired of stomaching untruths over here. We are downright getting angry over here"—the Senator was speaking from the other side of the aisle. Then with reference to the President again, the Senator said, "This guy is not going to tell the truth," and then proceeded to accuse the President "and many Senators"—"and many Senators"—of making statements that tax cuts have been targeted for the wealthy, "when they know that is a lie." Now, the Senator said, "I am using strong terms like 'lie.'" Then the Senator made reference to a lack of statesmanship: "When are we going to get statesmen again in this country? When are we going to get these statesmen here in Washington again?" And then answering his own question, he said, "they are here," presumably, one would suppose, referring to himself as one such statesman.

Mr. President, such statements are harsh and severe, to say the least. And when made by a Senator who has not yet held the office of Senator a full year, they are really quite astonishing. In my 37 years in this Senate, I do not recall such insolence, and it is very sad that debate and discourse on the Senate floor have sunk to such a low level. The Senator said, "We are downright getting angry over here." Now, what is that supposed to mean? Does it mean that we on this side should sit in fear and in trembling because someone is getting downright angry? Mr. President, those whom God wishes to destroy, he first makes mad. Solomon tells us: "He that is slow to anger is better than the mighty; and he that ruleth his spirit than he that taketh a city."

Moreover, Mr. President, for a Senator to make reference on the Senate floor to any President, Democrat or Republican as "this guy" is to show an utter disrespect for the office of the presidency itself, and is also to show an uncaring regard for the disrespect that the Senator brings upon himself as a result. "This guy is not going to tell the truth," the Senator said, and then he proceeded to state that the President "and many Senators" have made statements concerning tax cuts—and that would include almost all Senators on this side, because almost all of us have so stated—that "they know that is a lie,"—and I am quoting—that "they know that is a lie"—admitting, the Senator said, that the word "lie" is a strong term. I have never heard that word used in the Senate before in addressing other Senators. I have never heard other Senators called liars. I have never heard a Senator say that other Senators lie.

Mr. President, the use of such maledic[t] language on the Senate floor is quite out of place, and to accuse other Senators of being liars is to skate on very, very thin ice, indeed.

In his first of three epistles, John admonishes us: "He that saith, I know him, and keepeth not his commandments, is a liar, and the truth is not in him." Mr. President, it seems to me that by that standard, all of us are certainly—or certainly most of us— fall into the classification of liar, and before accusing other Senators of telling a lie, one should "cast first the beam out of thine own eye, and then shalt thou see clearly to pull out the mote that is in thy brother's eye."

Mr. President, can't we rein in our tongues and lower our voices and speak to each other and about each other in a more civil fashion? I can disagree with another Senator. I have done so many times in this Chamber. I can state that he is mistaken in his facts; I can state that he is in error. I can do all these things without assaulting his character by calling him a liar, by saying that he lies. Have civility and common courtesy and reasonableness taken leave of this Chamber? Surely the individual vocabularies of Members of this body have not deteriorated to the point that we can only express ourselves in such crude and coarse and offensive language. The proverb tells us that "A fool uttereth all his mind: but a wise man keepeth it in till afterwards." Can we no longer engage in reasoned, even intense, partisan exchanges in the Senate without imputing evil motives to other Senators, without castigating the personal integrity of our colleagues? Such utterly reckless statements can only poison the waters of the well of mutual respect and comity which must prevail in this body if our two political parties are to work together in the best interests of the people whom we serve. The work of the two Leaders, the work of Mr. DOLE the work of Mr. DASCHLE is thus made more difficult. There is enough controversy in the natural course of things in this bitter year, without making statements that stir even greater controversy and divisiveness.

"If a House be divided against itself, that House cannot stand," we are told in Mark's Gospel. Surely the people who see and hear the Senate at its worst must become discouraged and throw up their hands in disgust at hearing such sour inflammatory rhetoric, which exhales itself fuliginously. What can our young people think—they listen to C-SPAN; they watch C-SPAN. What can our young people think when they hear grown men in the premiere upper body among the world's legislatures casting such rash aspersions upon the President of the United States and upon other Senators? Political partisanship is to be expected in a legislative body—we all engage in it—but bitter personal attacks go beyond the pale of respectable propriety. And let us all be scrupulously mindful of the role that vitriolic public statements can play in the stirring of the dark cauldron of violent passions which are far too evident in our land today. Oklahoma City is but 8 months behind us. Washington, in his farewell address, warned against party and factional strife. In remarks such as those that were made last Friday, we are seeing bitter partisanship and factionalism at their worst. I hope that the leaders of our two parties will attempt to impress upon our colleagues the need to tone down the rhetoric and to avoid engaging in vicious diatribes that impugn and question the motives and principles and the personal integrity of other Senators and of the Presidency of United States.

It is one thing to criticize the policies of the President and his administration. I have offered my own strong criticism of President Clinton and past Presidents of both parties in respect to some of their policies. I simply do not agree with some of them. But it is quite another matter to engage in personal attacks that hold the President up to obloquy and opprobrium and scorn. Senators ought to be bigger than that. Anyone who thinks of himself as a gentleman ought to be above such contumely. The bandying about of such words as liar, or lie, can only come from a contumelious lip, and for one, who has been honored by the electorate to serve in the high office of United States Senator, to engage in such rude language arising from haughtiness and contempt, is to lower himself in the eyes of his peers, and of the American people generally, to the status of a steet brawler.

Mr. President, in 1863, Willard Saulsbury of Delaware, in lengthy remarks, referred to President Abraham Lincoln as a "weak and imbecile man" and accused other Senators of "blackguardism." Saulsbury was ruled out of order by the Vice President who sat in the Chair and ordered to take his seat. Another Senator ordered a resolution the following day for his expulsion, but Saulsbury appeared the next day and apologized to the Senate for his remarks, which were quite out of order, and that was the end of the matter. Senators should take note of this and try to restrain their indulgence for outlandish and extreme accusations and charges in public debate on this floor.

The kind of mindless gabble and rhetorical putridities as were voiced on this floor last Friday can only create bewilderment and doubt among the American people as to our ability to work with each other in this Chamber. And that is what they expect us to do. Certainly these are not the attributes and marks of a statesman. Statesmen do not call each other liars or engage in such execrations as fly from pillar to post in this Chamber. I have seen statesmen during my time in the Senate, and they have stood on both sides of the aisle. They have stood tall, suncrowned, and above the fog in public duty and in private thinking—above the fog of personal insinuations and malicious calumny.

The Bob Tafts, the Everett Dirksens—I have seen him stand at that desk—the Everett Dirksens, the Norris Cottons, George Aikens, the Howard Bakers, the Jack Javitses, the Hugh Scotts, or the John Heinzes of yesteryear did not throw the word "lie" in the teeth of their colleagues. Nor do such honorable colleagues who serve today as THAD COCHRAN, MARK HATFIELD, TED STEVENS, JOHN CHAFEE, ARLEN SPECTER, NANCY KASSEBAUM, BILL COHEN, ORRIN Hatch, JOHN WARNER, DIRK KEMPTHORNE, ALAN SIMPSON—oh, there is one I will miss when he leaves this Chamber—and many other Senators on that side of the aisle. BOB BENNETT of Utah recognized the rhetorical cesspool for what it was last Friday and he kept himself above it. He took note of it. I have never heard our majority leader, I have never heard our minority leader, I have never heard any majority leader or minority leader accuse other Senators of lying. I am confident that our leaders and most Senators find such gutter talk to be unacceptable in this forum.

Mr. President, in 1986, I helped to open the Senate floor to the televising of Senate debate. On the whole, I think it has worked rather well. I believed then and I still believe that TV coverage of Senate debate can and should educate and inspire the American people. But in my 37 years in the United States Senate, this has been a different year. William Manchester in his book "The Glory and the Dream" speaks of the year 1932 as the "cruelest year." I was a boy growing up in the Depression in 1932. I remember it as the cruelest year. But, Mr. President, in some ways, I think this year has been even more cruel. I have seen the Senate deteriorate this year. The decorum in the Senate has deteriorated, and political partisanship has run rife. And when the American people see and hear such intellectual pemmican as was spewed forth on this floor last Friday, no wonder there is such a growing disrespect for Congress throughout the country. The American people have every right to think that we are just a miserable lot of bickering juveniles, and I have come to be sorry that television is here, when we make such a spectacle of ourselves. When we accuse our colleagues of lying—I have never done that. I have never heard it done in this Senate before. Clay and John Randolph fought a duel over less than that. Aaron Burr shot and killed Alexander Hamilton for less than that. When we accuse our colleagues of lying and deliver ourselves of reckless imprecations and vengeful maledictions against the President of the United States, and against other Senators, it is no wonder—no wonder—that good men and women who have served honorably and long in this body are saying they have had enough! They may not go out here publicly and say that, but they have had enough.

Mr. President, it is with profound sadness that I have taken the Floor today to express my alarm and concern at the poison that has settled in upon this chamber. There have been giants in this Senate, and I have seen some of them. Little did I know when I came here that I would live to see pygmies stride like colossuses while marveling, like Aesop's fly, sitting on the axle of a chariot, "My, what a dust I do raise!"

Mr. President, party has a tendency to warp intelligence. I was chosen a Senator by a majority of the people of West Virginia seven times, but not for a party. I try to represent all of the people of the state—Democrats and Republicans—who sent me here. I recognize no claim upon my action in the name and for the sake of party only. The oath I have taken 13 times, and in my 50 years of public service, is to support and defend the Constitution of my country's government, not the fiat of any political organization. This is not to say that political party is not important. It is. But party is not all important. Many times I have said that there are several things that are more important than political party. Sometimes as I sit and listen to Senate debate, I get the impression that to some of us political party is above everything else. I sometimes get the impression that, more important than what serves the best interests of our country is what serves the political fortunes of a political party in the next elections. This Senate was not created for that purpose. This is not a forum that was created for the purpose of advancing one's political career or one's political party. In the day that the Senate was created, no such thing as political party in the United States was even a consideration. None of our forebears who created our republican form of government was a party, but all were for the state. Political parties were formed afterward and have grown in strength since, and today the troubles that afflict our country, in many ways, chiefly may be said to arise from the dangerous excess of party feeling in our national councils. What does reason avail, when party spirit presides?

The welfare of the country is more dear than the mere victory of party. As George William Curtis once said, some may scorn this practical patriotism as impracticable folly. But such was the folly of the Spartan Leonidas, holding back, with his 300, the Persian horde, and teaching Greece the self reliance that saved her. Such was the folly of the Swiss Arnold von Winkelried, gathering into his own breast the points of Austrian spears, making his dead body the bridge of victory for his countrymen. Such was the folly of Nathan Hale, who, on September 22, 1776, gladly risked the seeming disgrace of his name and grieved that he had but one life to give for his country. Such was the folly of Davy Crockett and 182 other defenders of the Alamo who were slain after holding out 13 days against a Mexican army in 1836, thus pemitting Sam Houston time enough to perfect plans for the defense of Texas. Such are the beacon lights of a pure patriotism that burn forever in men's memories and shine forth brightly through the illuminated ages. What has happened to all of that?

Mr. President, when our forefathers were blackened by the smoke and grime at Shiloh and at Fredericksburg, they did not ask or care whether those who stood shoulder to shoulder beside them were Democrats or Republicans; they asked only that they might prove as true as was the steel in the rifles that they grasped in their hands. The cannonballs that mowed brave men down like stalks of corn were not labeled Republican cannonballs or Democrat cannonballs. When those intrepid soldiers fought with unfailing loyalty to General Thomas J. Jackson—who was born in what is now Harrison County, West Virginia—who stood like a wall of stone in the midst of shot and shell at the first battle of Bull Run, they did not ask each other whether that brave officer, who later fell the victim of a rifle ball, was a Democrat or Republican. They did not pause to question the politics of that cool gunner standing by his smoking cannon in the midst of death, whether the poor wounded, mangled, gasping comrades, crushed and torn, and dying in agony all about them—had voted for Lincoln or Douglas, for Breckinridge or Bell. No. They were full of other thoughts. Men were prized for what they were worth to the common country of us all, not for the party to which they belonged. The bones that molder today beneath the sod in Flanders Field and in Arlington Cemetery do not sleep in graves that are Republican or Democrat. These are Americans who gave their lives in the service of their country, not in the service of a political party. We who serve together in this Senate, must know this in our hearts.

I understand, and we understand, that partisanship plays a part in our work here. There is nothing inherently wrong with that. There is nothing inherently wrong with partisanship. But I hope that we will all take a look at ourselves on both sides of this aisle and understand also that we must work together in harmony and with mutual respect for one another. This very charter of government under which we live was created in a spirit of compromise and mutual concession. And it is only in that spirit that a continuance of this charter of government can be prolonged and sustained. When the Committee on Style and Revision of the Federal Convention of 1787 had prepared a digest of their plan, they reported a letter to accompany the plan to Congress, from which I take these words: "And thus the Constitution which we now present is the result of a spirit of amity and of that mutual deference and concession which the peculiarity of our political situation rendered indispensable."

Mr. President, Majorian, the Emperor of the West, in 457 A.D. said he was a prince "who still gloried in the name of Senator."

Mr. President, as one who has gloried in the name of Senator, I shudder to think of the day when, because of the shamelessness and reckless intemperance of a few, I might instead become one who is embarrassed by it.

Let us stop this seemingly irresistible urge to destroy all that we have always held sacred. Let us cease this childish need to resort to emotional strip-tease on the Senate Floor.

Let us remember that we are lucky enough to reside in the greatest country on earth and to have the further fortune to have been selected by the American people to actively participate as their representatives in this miraculous experiment in freedom which has set the world afire with hope.

Mr. President, there are rules of the Senate and we simply cannot ignore those rules. We must defend them and cherish them. I will read to the Senate what Vice President Adlai E. Stevenson said with regard to the Senate's rules on March 3, 1897, because I believe his observation is as fitting today as it was at the end of the 19th century:

It must not be forgotten that the rules governing this body are founded deep in human experience; that they are the result of centuries of tireless effort in legislative hall, to conserve, to render stable and secure, the rights and liberties which have been achieved by conflict. By its rules the Senate wisely fixes the limits to its own power. Of those who clamor against the Senate, and its methods of procedure, it may be truly said: "They know not what they do." In this Chamber alone are preserved, without restraint, two essentials of wise legislation and of good government—the right of amendment and of debate. Great evils often result from hasty legislation; rarely from the delay which follows full discussion and deliberation. In my humble judgment, the historic Senate—preserving the unrestricted right of amendment and of debate, maintaining intact, the time-honored parliamentary methods and amenities which unfailingly secure action after deliberation—possesses in our scheme of government a value which cannot be measured by words.

Mr. President, we must honor these rules. The distinguished Presiding Officer today, SLADE GORTON of Washington, respects and honors these rules. We simply have to stop this business of castigating the integrity of other Senators. We all have to abide by these rules.

Mr. President, may a temperate spirit return to this chamber and may it again reign in our public debates and political discourses, that the great eagle in our national seal may continue to look toward the sun with piercing eyes that survey, with majestic grace, all who come within the scope and shadow of its mighty wings.

I yield the floor.

II. NATURE OF GOVERNMENT

A GOVERNMENT THAT HELPS PEOPLE HELP THEMSELVES[1]
WILLIAM J. CLINTON

President of the United States; born 1947, Hope, AR; B.S., George-town University, 1968; Rhodes Scholar, Oxford University, 1968–70; J.D., Yale University, 1973; Governor of Arkansas, 1979–81, 1983–92.

Editors' introduction: On April 25, 1995, President Clinton addressed members of the Iowa State Legislature, Iowa Supreme Court state officials, and guests at the State Capital in Des Moines. Five days later the Oklahoma City bombing found 165 people dead, 467 injured, and two missing. Peter Applebome (*New York Times* April 23, 1995) explained how "hatred of the Federal Government and issues like gun control have replaced race as the issues that bind members of the Patriot Movement." In addition to praising Oklahoma City citizens for responding to the needs of those suffering from the bombing, and assessing causes of social unrest in America, Clinton cautioned all citizens that "words have consequences." As the editors illustrate in the Preface of this volume, a "clash of cultures" took place during 1995–1996 and earlier over what should be the size, nature, and function of federal government. In the speech below, Clinton envisioned the kind of government required for "a new and different world."

William J. Clinton's speech: Thank you very much, Mr. President, Mr. Speaker, Governor Branstad, Mr. Chief Justice, and members of the Supreme Court, distinguished Iowa state officials. And former Congressman Neil Smith, my good friend, and Mrs. Smith, thank you for being here. To all of you who are members of the Iowa legislature, House and Senate, Republican and Democrat, it is a great honor for me to be here today.

[1]Delivered at the the State Capital in Des Moines, IA, on April 25, 1995 at 7:32 p.m.

I feel that I'm back home again. When I met the legislative leadership on the way in and we shared a few words and then they left to come in here, and I was standing around with my crowd, I said, you know, I really miss state government. (Laughter.) I'll say more about why in a moment. (Laughter.)

I'd like to, if I might, recognize one of your members to thank him for agreeing to join my team—Representative Running will now be the Secretary of Labor's representative. (Applause.) Would you stand up, please. (Applause.) Thank you.

Representative Running is going to be the representative of the Secretary of Labor for region 7—Iowa, Nebraska, Missouri and Kansas. And if you will finish your business here pretty soon, he can actually go to Kansas City and get to work—(laughter)—which I would appreciate.

I'm delighted to be back in Iowa. I had a wonderful day here, and it was good to be here when it was dry—(laughter)—although a little rain doesn't do any harm.

We had a wonderful meeting today at Iowa State University with which I'm sure all of you are familiar, this National Rural Conference we had, designed to lay the groundwork for a strategy for rural America to include not only the farm bill, but also a rural development strategy and a strategy generally to deal with the problems of rural America—with the income disparities with the rest of America, the age disparities with the rest of America, and the problems of getting services and maintaining the quality of life in rural America.

I want to thank Governor Branstad for his outstanding presentation and the information he gave us about the efforts being made in Iowa in developing your fiber optic network and developing the health care reform initiatives for rural Iowans and many other areas. I want to thank Senator Harkin for his presentation, particularly involving the development of alternative agricultural products as a way to boost income in rural America. And I want to say a special word of thanks to the people at Iowa State. They did a magnificent job there, and I know you are all very proud of that institution, and you would have been very, very proud of them today, the way they performed.

I'm also just glad to be back here in the setting of state government. You know, Governor Branstad and I were once the youngest governors in America, but time took care of it. (Laughter.) And now that he's been reelected, he will actually serve more years than I did. I ran for a fifth term as governor. We used to have two-year terms, and then we switched to four-year terms. And only one person in the history of our state had ever served more than eight years, and only one person had ever served more than—two people had served more than two terms, but those were two-year terms—in the whole history of the state. So I was—I had served 10 years. I'd served three two year terms and one four-year term, and I was . . . attempting to be reelected. And I had a high job approval rating, but people were reluctant to vote for me, because in my state people are very suspicious of too much political power, you know. And I thought I was still pretty young and healthy, but half of them wanted to give me a gold watch, you know, and send me home. (Laughter.)

And I never will forget one day when I was running for my fifth term, I was out at the State Fair doing governor's day at the State Fair, which I always did, and I would just sit there and anybody that wanted to talk to me could up and say whatever was on their mind, which was, for me a hazardous undertaking from time to time—(laughter)—since they invariably would do exactly that. And I stayed there all day long, and I talked about everything under the moon and sun with the people who came up and, long about the end of the day, this elderly fellow in overalls came up to me and he said, Bill, you going to run for governor, again? And I hadn't announced yet. I said, I don't know. If I do, will you vote for me? He said, yes, I always have. I guess I will again. And I said, well, aren't you sick of me after all these years? He said, no, but everybody else I know is.

But he went on to say—and that's the point I want to make about state government—he said, people get tired of it because all you do is nag us. You nag us to modernize the economy, you nag us to improve the schools, you just nag, nag, nag. But he said, I think it's beginning to work. And what I have seen in state after state after state over the last 15 years as we have gone through these wrenching economic and social changes in America and as we face challenge after challenge after challenge, is people able consistently to come together to overcome their differences, to focus on what it will take to build a state and to move forward. And we need more of that in America.

In Iowa, you do embody our best values. People are independent, but committed to one another. They work hard and play by the rules, but they work together. Those of us who come from small towns understand that everybody counts. We don't have a person to waste. And the fact that Iowa has done such a good job in developing all of your people is one of the reasons that you are so strong in every single national indicator of success that I know of. And you should be very, very proud of what, together, you have done. (Applause.)

I saw some of that American spirit in a very painful way in Oklahoma City this week, and all of you saw it as well. I know you share the grief of the people there. But you must also share the pride of all Americans in seeing the enormity of the effort which is being exerted there, by firemen and police officers, and nurses, by rescue workers, by people who have come from all over America and given up their lives to try to help Oklahoma City and the people there who have suffered so much loss rebuild.

I want to say again what I have tried to say for the last three days to the American people. On this National Day of Service, there is a service we can do to ensure that we build on, and learn from, this experience.

We must always fight for the freedom of speech. The First Amendment, with its freedom of speech, freedom of assembly and freedom of worship, is the essence of what it means to be an American. And I dare say every elected official in this room would give his or her life to preserve that right for our children and our grandchildren down to the end of time.

But we have to remember that that freedom has endured in our nation for over 200 years because we practiced it with such responsibility; because we had discipline; because we understood from the Founding Fathers forward that you could not have very, very wide latitude in personal freedom until you also had, or unless you also had, great discipline in the exercise of that freedom.

So while I would defend to the death anyone's right to the broadest freedom of speech, I think we should all remember that words have consequences. And freedom should be exercised with responsibility. And when we think that others are exercising their freedom in an irresponsible way, it is our job to stand up and say that is wrong. We disagree. This is not a matter of partisan politics. It is not a matter of political philosophy. If we see the freedom of expression and speech abused in this country, whether it comes from the right or the left, from the media or from people just speaking on their own, we should stand up and say no, we don't believe in preaching violence; we don't believe in preaching

GOSHEN COLLEGE LIBRARY
GOSHEN, INDIANA

hatred; we don't believe in preaching discord. Words have consequences.

If words did not have consequences, we wouldn't be here today. We're here today because Patrick Henry's words had consequences, because Thomas Jefferson's words had consequences, because Abraham Lincoln's words had consequences. And these words we hear today have consequences—the good ones and the bad ones, the ones that bring us together, and the ones that drive a wedge through our heart.

We never know in this society today who is out there dealing with all kinds of inner turmoil, vulnerable to being pushed over the edge if all they hear is a relentless clamor of hatred and division. So let us preserve free speech, but let those of us who want to fight to preserve free speech forever in America say, we must be responsible and we will be. (Applause.)

My fellow Americans, I come here tonight, as I went recently to the state legislature in Florida, to discuss the condition of our country, where we're going in the future, and your role in that. We know we are in a new and different world—the end of the Cold War, a new and less organized world we're living in, but one still not free of threats. We know we have come to the end of an industrial age and we're in an information age, which is less bureaucratic, more open, more dependent on technology, more full of opportunity but still full of its own problems, than the age that most of us were raised in.

We know that we no longer need the same sort of bureaucratic, top-down, service-delivering, rule-making, centralized government in Washington that served us so well during the industrial age, because times have changed. We know that with all the problems we have and all the opportunities we have, we have to think anew about what the responsibilities of our government in Washington should be, what your responsibility should be here at the state level, and through you to the local level, and what should be done more by private citizens on their own with no involvement from the government.

We know now what the central challenge of this time is, and you can see it in Iowa. You could see it today with the testimony we heard at the Rural Conference. We are at a 25-year low in the combined rates of unemployment and inflation. Our economy has produced over 6 million new jobs. But paradoxically, even in Iowa where the unemployment rate has dropped under 3.5 per-

cent, most Americans are working harder today for the same or
lower incomes that they were making 10 years ago. And many
Americans feel less job security even as the recovery continues.

That is largely a function of the global economic competition,
the fact that technology raises productivity at an almost unbelievable rate so fewer and fewer people can do more and more work,
and that depresses wages. The fact that unless we raise it in Washington next year, the minimum wage will reach a 40-year low.

There are a lot of these things that are related one to the other. But it is perfectly clear that the economics are changing the
face of American society. You can see it in the difference in income in rural America and urban America. You can see it in the
difference—the aging process in rural America as compared with
urban America. And if we want to preserve the American Dream,
we have got to find a way to solve this riddle.

I was born in the year after World War II at the dawn of the
greatest explosion of opportunity in American history and in
world history. For 30 years after that, the American people, without regard to their income or region, grew and grew together.
That is, each income group over the next 30 years roughly doubled their income, except the poorest 20 percent of us that had
an almost 2.5 times increase in their income. So we were growing
and growing together.

For about the last 15 or 20 years, half of us have been stuck
so that our country is growing, but we are growing apart even
within the middle class. When you put that beside the fact that
we have more and more poor people who are not elderly—which
was the case when I was little, but now are largely young women
and their little children, often where there was either no marriage or the marriage is broken up so there is not a stable home
and there is not an adequate level of education to ensure an income—you have increasing poverty and increasing splits within
the middle class. That is the fundamental cause, I believe, of a lot
of the problems that we face in America and a lot of the anxiety
and frustration we see in this country.

Every rich country faces this problem. But in the United
States, it is a particular problem—both because the inequality is
greater and because it violates the American Dream. I mean, this
is a country where if you work hard and you play by the rules, you
obey the law, you raise your children, you do your best to do
everything you're supposed to do, you ought to have an opportunity for the free enterprise system to work for you.

And so we face this challenge. I have to tell you that I believe two things: One, the future is far more hopeful than worrisome. If you look at the resources of this country, the assets of this country, and you compare them with any other country in the world, and you image what the world will be like 20 or 30 years from now, you'd have to be strongly bullish on America. You have to believe in our promise.

Secondly, I am convinced we cannot get there unless we develop a new way of talking about these issues, a new political discourse. Unless we move beyond the labeling that so often characterizes, and in fact mischaracterizes, the debate in Washington, D.C.

Now we are having this debate in ways that affect you, so you have to be a part of it, because one of the biggest parts of the debate is, how are we going to keep the American Dream alive? How are we going to keep America, the world's strongest force for freedom and democracy, into the next century, and change the way the government works?

There is broad consensus that the government in Washington should be less bureaucratic, less oriented toward rule-making, smaller, more flexible, that more decisions should be devolved to the state and local government level, and where possible, more decisions should be given to private citizens themselves. There is a broad agreement on that.

The question is, what are the details? What does that mean? What should we do? What should you do? That's what I want to talk to you about. There are clearly some national responsibilities, clearly some that would be better served here at your level.

The main reason I ran for President is, it seemed to me that we were seeing a national government in bipartisan gridlock, where we'd had 12 years in which we exploded the deficit, reduced our investment in people, and undermined our ability to compete and win in the world. And I wanted very badly to end the kind of gridlock we'd had and to see some real concrete action taken to go forward, because of my experience doing what you're doing now.

My basic belief is that the government ought to do more to help people help themselves, to reward responsibility with more opportunity, and not to give anybody opportunity without demanding responsibility. That's basically what I think our job is.

I think we can be less bureaucratic. We have to enhance security at home and abroad. But the most important thing we have to do is to empower people to make the most of their own lives.

Now, we have made a good beginning at that. As I said, we've been able to get the deficit down. You know here in Iowa, because you're a farming state, that we've had the biggest expansion of trade in the last two years we've seen in a generation. We now have a $20 billion surplus in agricultural products for the first time ever—this means more to me than you—but we're selling rice to the Japanese, something that my farmers never thought that we'd ever do. We're selling apples in Asia. We are doing our best in Washington—some of us are —to get the ethanol program up and going. This administration is for it, and I hope you will help us with that. (Applause.)

And we're making modest efforts which ought to be increased to work with the private sector to develop alternative agricultural products. Today I saw corn-based windshield wiper fluid, and something that I think is important, biodegradable, agriculturally-rooted golf tees. (Laughter.) And a lot of other things that I think will be the hallmark of our future. We have only scratched the surface of what we can do to produce products from the land, from our food and fiber, and we must do more.

In education we are beginning to see the outlines of what I hope will be a genuine bipartisan national partnership in education. In the last two years we increased Head Start, we reduced the rules and regulations the federal government imposes on local school systems, but gave them more funds and flexibility to meet national standards of education. We helped states all over the country to develop comprehensive systems of apprenticeships for young people who get out of high school and don't want to go to college, but don't want to be in dead-end jobs.

We are doing more to try to make our job training programs relevant. And we have made literally millions of Americans eligible for lower cost, better repayment college loans under our direct loan program, including over 350,000 students and former students in Iowa—including all those who are at Iowa State University. Now, if you borrow money under that program, you get it quicker with less paperwork at lower cost, and you can pay it back in one of four different ways based on the income you're going to earn when you get out of college. Believe it or not, it lowers costs to the taxpayers.

And we have demanded responsibility. We've taken the loan default costs to the taxpayers from $2.8 billion a year down to $1 billion a year. That is the direction we ought to be going in.

We've worked hard to increase our security at home and abroad. The crime bill, which was passed last year by the Congress after six years of endless debate, provides for 100,000 more police officers on our street. We have already—over the next five years—we've already awarded over 17,000 police officers to over half the police departments in America, including 158 communities here in Iowa. It strengthens punishment under federal law.

The three strikes and you're out law in the crime bill is now the law of the land. The first person to be prosecuted under this law was a convicted murderer accused of an armed robbery in Waterloo last November. If he's convicted, he will go to jail for the rest of his life. (Applause.)

The capital punishment provisions of the crime bill will cover the incident in Oklahoma City—something that is terribly important, in my view, not only to bring justice in this case, but to send a clear signal that the United States does not intend to be dominated and paralyzed by terrorists from at home or abroad—not now, not ever. We cannot ever tolerate that. (Applause.)

We are also more secure from beyond our borders. For the first time since the dawn of the nuclear age, there are no Russian missiles pointed at America's children. And those nuclear weapons are being destroyed every day. (Applause.)

We have reduced the size of the federal government by more than 100,000. We are taking it down by more than a quarter of a million. We have eliminated or reduced 300 programs. And I have asked Congress to eliminate or consolidate 400 more. We have tried to give more flexibility to states—several states have gotten broad freedom from federal rules to implement health care reform. And we have now freed 27 states from cumbersome federal rules to try to help them end welfare as we know it.

In the almost two years since Iowa received only the second welfare waiver our administration issued, the number of welfare recipients in Iowa who hold jobs is almost doubled from 18 to 33 percent. You are doing it without punishing children for the mistakes of their parents—and I want to say more on that later—but you are doing it. And that is clear evidence that we should give the states the right to pursue welfare reform. They know how to get the job done better than the federal government has done in the past. We should give you all more responsibility for moving people from welfare to work. (Applause.)

Now, here's where you come in, because I want to talk in very short order, one right after the other, about the decisions we still have to make in Washington. Do we still have to cut the federal deficit more? Yes, we do. We've taken it down by $600 billion. The budget, in fact, would be balanced today if it weren't for the interest we have to pay on the debt run up between 1981 and 1992.

But it's still a problem and you need to understand why it's a problem. It's a problem because a lot of people who used to give us money to finance our government deficit and our trade deficit, need their money at home now. That's really what's happening in Japan. They need their money at home now.

We must continue—we must say to the world, to the financial markets—we will not cut taxes except in the context of reducing the deficit. America is committed. Both parties are committed. Americans are committed to getting rid of this terrible burden on our future. We must continue to do it.

Now, the question is, how are we going to do that? Should we cut unnecessary spending? Of course, we should. How do you define it? Should there be more power to state and local governments and to the private sector? You bet. But what are the details?

In other words, what we've got to do in Washington now is what you do all the time. We've got to move beyond our rhetoric to reality. And I think it would be helpful for you because we need your voice to be heard. And at least my experience in the Governors Association was, or working in my own legislature was, that on these issues we could get Republicans and Democrats together. So let me go through what we've done, and what's still to be done.

First of all, I agree with this new Congress on three issues that were in the Republican Contract—and two of them are already law. Number one, Congress should apply to itself all the laws it puts on the private sector. We should know when we make laws in Washington what we're doing to other people by experiencing it ourself. That was a good thing.

Number two, I signed the unfunded mandates legislation to make it harder, but not impossible when it [is] important, but much harder, for Congress to put on you and your taxpayers unfunded mandates from the federal government where we make you pay for something that we in Washington want to do. I strongly support that, and I think all of you do, as well.

The third thing we are doing that we have not finished yet, although both Houses have approved a version of it, is the line-item veto. Almost every governor has it. I don't want to embarrass anybody here, but I don't know how many times I had a legislature say, now, Governor, I'm going to slip this in this bill because I've got to do it, and then you can scratch it out for me. (Laughter.) And it was fine. We did it. (Laughter.) Now if they slip it in a bill, I have to decide what to do or not. I have to decide.

When the farmers in Iowa desperately needed the restoration of the tax deduction for health insurance, the 25 percent tax deduction that self-employed farmers and others get for health insurance, there was a provision of that bill I didn't like very much. I had to decide, am I going to give this back to 3.3 million self-employed Americans and their families, to lower the cost of health care by tax day, or not? But when we have the line-item veto, it won't be that way. And we need it.

Here are the hard ones. Number one, the farm bill. Should [w]e reduce farm supports? Yes, we should, as required by GATT. I worked hard to get the Europeans to the table in agriculture in this trade agreement. A lot of you understand that. The deal was, they would reduce their subsidies more than we would reduce ours, so we would at least move toward some parity, so that our farmers would get a fair break for a change. Now some say, let's just get rid of all these farm support programs.

Well, if we do it now, we give our competitors the advantage we worked for eight years to take away. We put family farms more at risk. Now if anybody's got better ideas about what should be in the Farm Bill, that's fine. If anybody's got a better idea about how to save the family farmers, let's do it. If anybody has new ideas about what should be put in for rural development, fine. But let us do no harm. Let us not labor under the illusion that having fought so hard to have a competitive agricultural playing field throughout the world, having achieved a $20 billion surplus in agriculture, we can turn and walk away from the farmers of the country in the name of cutting spending. That is not the way to cut the federal deficit. (Applause.)

I'll give you another example. Some believe that we should flat fund the school lunch program. And then there's a big argument in Washington, is it a cut or not. Let me tell you something, all these block grants are designed not only to give you more flexibility, but to save the federal government money. Now it may be a good deal, or it may not. You have to decide. But when we wanted to cut the Agriculture Department budget—we're closing nearly 1,200 offices, we're reducing employment by 13,000, we eliminated 14 divisions in the Department of Agriculture—my own view is, that is better than putting an arbitrary cap on the school lunch program, which will be terribly unfair to the number—to the numerous school districts in this country that have increasing burdens from low income children. There are a lot of kids in this country—a lot of kids—the only decent meal they get every day is the meal they get at school. This program works. If it's not broke, we shouldn't fix it. So I don't agree with that. But you have to decide.

Welfare reform. I've already said, we have now given more welfare reform waivers to states to get out from under the federal government than were given in the last 12 years put together. In two years, we've given more than 12 years. I am for you figuring out how you want to run you[r] welfare system and move people from welfare to work. I am for that.

But here are the questions. Number one, should we have cumbersome federal rules that say you have to penalize teenage girls who give birth to children and cut them off? I don't think so. We should never punish children for the mistakes of their parents. And these children who become parents prematurely, we should say, you made a mistake, you shouldn't do that—no child should do that. But what we're going to do is impose responsibilities on you for the future, to make you a responsible parent, a responsible student, a responsible worker. That's what your program does. Why should the federal government tell you that you have to punish children, when what you really want to do is move people from welfare to work so that more people are good parents and good workers. You should decide that. We do not need to be giving you lectures about how you have to punish the kids of this country. We need a welfare bill that is tough on work and compassionate toward children—not a welfare bill that is weak on work and tough on children. I feel that that should be a bipartisan principle that all of us should be able to embrace.

Now, the second issue in welfare reform is whether we should give you a block grant. Instead of having the welfare being an individual entitlement to every poor person on welfare, should we just give you whatever money we gave you last year or over the last three years and let you spend it however you want? There are two issues here that I ask you to think about, not only from your perspective, but from the perspective of every other state.

In Florida, the Republicans in legislature I spoke with were not for this. And here's why. The whole purpose of the block grant is twofold. One is, we give you more flexibility. The second is, we say in return for more flexibility, you ought to be able to do the job for less money, so we won't increase the money you're getting over the next five years, which means we'll get to save money and lower the deficit. If it works for everybody concerned it's a good deal.

But what are the states—there are two problems with a block grant in this area, and I want you to help me work through it, because I am for more flexibility for the states. I would give every state every waiver that I have given to any state. I want you to decide what to do with this. I want you to be out there creating innovative ways to break the cycle of welfare dependency.

But there are two problems with this. Number one, if you have a state with a very large number of children eligible for public assistance and they're growing rapidly, it's very hard to devise any formula that keeps you from getting hurt in the block grants over a five-year period. And some states have rapidly growing populations—Florida, Texas, probably California.

Number two, a total block grant relieves the state of any responsibility to put up the match that is now required for you to participate in the program. Now, you may say, well, we would do that anyway. We have a tradition in Iowa of taking care of our own. But what if you lived in a state with a booming population growth, with wildly competing demands for dollars? And what about when the next recession comes? Keep in mind, we're making all these decisions today in the second year in which every state economy is growing. That has not happened in a very long time.

Will that really be fair? How do you know that there won't be insurmountable pressure in some states just to say, well, we can't take care of these children anymore; we've got to give the money to our school teachers; we've got to give the money to our road program; we've got to give the money to economic development; we've got environmental problems. So I ask you to think about those things. We can find a way to let you control the welfare system and move people from welfare to work, but there are two substantive problems with the block grant program that I want to see overcome before I sign off on it, because there is a national responsibility to care for the children of the country, to make sure a minimal standard of care is given. (Applause.) Thank you. (Applause.)

In the crime bill, there is a proposal to take what we did last time, which was to divide the money between police, prisons and prevention, and basically give you a block grant in prevention, and instead create two separate block grants, one for prisons and one for police and prevention, in which you would reduce the amount of money for police and prevention and increase the amount of money for prisons, but you could only get it if you decided—a mandate, but a funded one—if you decided to make all people who committed serious crimes serve 85 percent of their sentences.

So Washington is telling you how you have to sentence people but offering you money to build prisons. The practical impact means that a lot of that money won't be taken care of, and we will reduce the amount of money we're spending for police and for prevention programs. I think that's a mistake.

I'm more than happy for you to have block grants for prevention programs. You know more about what keeps kids out of jail and off the streets and from committing crime in Des Moines or Cedar Rapids or Ames or any place else than I would ever know. But we do know that the violent crime rate has tripled in the last 30 years, and the number of police on our street has only gone up by 10 percent. And we know there is city, after city, after city in America where the crime rate has gone down a lot, a lot when police have been put on the street in community policing roles.

So I say, let's keep the 100,000 police program. It is totally nonbureaucratic. Small towns in Iowa can get it by filling out a one-page, eight-question form. There is no hassle. And we should do this because we know it works. There is a national interest in safer streets, and it's all paid for by reducing the federal bureaucracy. So my view is, keep the 100,000 police, give the states flexibility on prevention. And I hope that you will agree with that. That, at any rate, is my strong feeling.

Lastly, let me say on education, I simply don't believe that we should be cutting education to reduce the deficit or pay for tax cuts. (Applause.) I don't believe that. I just don't believe that. (Applause.)

So my view—my view on this is that the way to save money is to give every university in the country and every college in the country the right to do what Iowa State has done—go to the direct loan program, cut out the middle man, lower the cost of loans, save the taxpayer money.

I am strongly opposed to charging the students interest on their student loans while they're in college. That will add 18 to 20 percent to the cost of education for a lot of our young people. We'll have fewer people going to school. We want more people going to school. I think that is a mistake.

I believe if we're going to have a tax cut, it should be targeted to middle class people and to educational needs. I believe strongly we should do two things more than anything else. Number one, give more people the advantage of an IRA, which they can put money into and save and then withdraw to pay for education or health care costs, purchase of a first-time home, or care of an elderly parent tax-free. Number two, allow the deduction of the cost of education after high school to all American middle-class families. (Applause.) Now, that, I think, will make a difference. (Applause.)

This is very important for you because, remember, we have a smaller total tax cut, if we target it to the middle class, we can have deficit reduction without cutting education. We can have deficit reduction without having severe cuts in Medicare. Governor Branstad said today, one of our biggest problems is the unfairness of the distribution of Medicare funds. You are right. It's not fair to rural America. But there's a lot more coming, and more than you need to have if we have an excessive tax cut that is not targeted to education and to the middle class.

So that, in brief, is the laundry list of the new federalism—the things you need to decide on. I do not believe these issues I have spoken with you about have a partisan tinge in Des Moines. They need not have one in Washington.

But I invite you, go back home—this is being televised tonight—go back home and talk to the people you represent, and ask them what they want you to say to your members of Congress about what we do in Washington; what you do in Des Moines; what we do in our private lives; what should be spent to reduce the deficit; what should be spent on a tax cut; what should be in a block grant; and where should we stand up and say we've got to protect the children of the country. These are great and exciting issues.

Believe me, if we make the right decisions—if we make the right decisions, the 21st century will still be the American century.

Thank you all, and God bless you. (Applause.)

PROMISES KEPT: CONTROLLING GOVERNMENT[2]
Rod Grams

United States Senator, Minnesota; born Princeton, MN, 1948; Anoka-Ramsey Junior College, Brown Institute in Minneapolis, and Carroll College, Helena, Montana; U.S. House of Representatives, 1992–95; producer and news anchor, TV stations in Minneapolis/St. Paul, Great Falls, Montana, Wausau, Wisconsin, and Rockford, Illinois; employed in solar energy and construction.

Editors' introduction: Senator Rod Grams, Republican from Minnesota, serves on the Senate committees of Banking, Housing, and Urban Affairs; Energy and Natural Resources; and Foreign Relations. In the U.S. Senate, on January 23, 1996, Grams and Craig Thomas of Wyoming reported on the tour they and seven other freshman Senators made a week earlier. Thomas described how they began in Washington, and continued through the Midwest, ending in Cheyenne, Wyoming. The theme of their rhetorical excursion was, "Promises Made, Promises Kept." They "made 10 stops in 9 States to talk about the commitment to the things that had brought us to the Senate in 1994." In Cheyenne "we had the largest town meeting we have ever had there. Feeling some kinship in that we have come here together, we were committed to change," Thomas explained, their message being that "the Federal Government is too big and costs too much and we need to change the regulatory restrictions on the opportunities in this country." Thomas contended that, on their tour, instead of the usual "politics by posturing . . . and perception, and governing by advertising and spinning," they introduced facts. "While we have not accomplished . . . all . . . that we would like

[2]Delivered at the United States Senate, Washington, D.C., on January 23, 1996.

to [in the Congress,] the major change has been the turn of the debate." Instead of discussing "how much more money to put into Lyndon Johnson Great Society programs," Thomas concluded that Republican conservatives are talking "about . . . reducing spending . . . a balanced budget . . . entitlement changes . . . middle income tax reform . . . lower interest rates."

During the year, even Republican leaders had difficulty bridling the independent freshman Republican members of the Senate and House. Concerned that they might convey a negative television image of their Party, Republican leaders coached "feisty House freshmen to avoid groan[ing] over any factually challenged statements" they judged President Clinton to make in his nationally televised State of the Union speech, January 23, 1996 (Katharine Q. Seelye, *New York Times*, Jan. 23, 1966).

In the speech below, Grams provides further explanation and details of the freshmen's "whirlwind" tour. By March 24, 1996, two months after the freshman Senators' tour, columnist Michael Wines (*New York Times*) found evidence that, at least in the U.S. House, the seventy-three Republican freshmen, who formerly had been "uncompromising and anti-politicians in their stances, in recent weeks, had decided that being right has sometimes meant being less far-right, and less inflexible."

Rod Grams's speech: Mr. President, too often here in Washington, politicians come to town with a mission but end up coming down with a severe case of Beltway fever.

They get caught up in the unreal atmosphere of this place and eventually forget what it was that first propelled them into public service.

They shut themselves away in their Senate or House offices or even in the Oval Office.

They spend their time hobnobbing with their new-found Washington friends. And after awhile, they just lose touch with the folks who sent them here. They think they are doing "the people's business," but in truth, they are no longer speaking for the people at all.

The 11 Members of the Senate freshman class came to town with a mission, too, a mandate given to us by the voters.

We met often as a group last year to track our progress. And as 1995 came to a close, we took a step back and began asking ourselves some pretty tough questions, such as:

What is the mood of the country?

What are people saying about Congress and the decisions we freshmen faced in our first year in the Senate?

Did we really hear the message we thought we heard in November 1994, when the voters sent us here to balance the budget to get Government spending under control, to deliver middle-class tax relief, and protect and strengthen Medicare and Medicaid?

Most importantly, is the message that brought this freshman class to the Senate in 1994 still alive and well in 1996?

We thought we knew the answers, and we knew we had delivered on each one of our promises, but after being in Washington and of course, debating those very important questions over the past year, we thought it was time for a reality check.

So last week, at the urging of my good friend, Senator Abraham from Michigan, nine Members of the freshman class took to the road to take our message directly to the people and bring the people's message back with us to Washington.

We visited eight cities over 4 days. What we saw and heard truly opened our eyes and, I believe, reaffirmed our mission.

In Philadelphia, we toured an empowerment zone and shared ideas on how to rebuild our troubled inner cities. The section of north Philadelphia we visited is a model for the concept that restoring neighborhoods means creating incentives for businesses to locate in urban areas. The Federal Government has made a difference, local officials told us, but the incentive is tax relief for these areas to attract businesses and jobs.

In Knoxville, 300 concerned citizens packed the auditorium at West High School for a town meeting. They cheered our progress on a balanced budget and called on us—and forcefully I might add—not to give up.

In Columbus, at a crime forum, we met with police, other law-enforcement officials, and victims of crime who shared how Washington can play an important role in making local neighborhoods safer.

Rain, sleet, snow, and even a blizzard warning could not stop a crowd from attending my town meeting in Minneapolis. We had a frank and, I believe, lively discussion covering a tremendous range of issues and the audience enthusiastically applauded our efforts to shrink the size and scope of government and return power to the States.

Employees at the Emerson Electric Co. in St. Louis sat down with us to talk about a balanced budget and just what it would mean for themselves and their families. It was heartening to hear their words of support, especially since our budget is specifically targeted at improving their lives, and the lives of every hard-working, taxpaying, middle-class American family.

In Tulsa, we met with small business owners—the men and women who create the jobs on Main Street—for a roundtable discussion organized by the Metropolitan Tulsa Chamber of Commerce.

Again, they thanked the Members of the 109th Congress for taking such a strong lead in bringing job providers relief from the stranglehold of Federal regulations and mandates.

Our whirlwind tour ended in Cheyenne, with a final opportunity to hear from the voters at a town hall meeting at the Cheyenne Civic Center.

At each stop, the people thanked us for taking our message directly to them and bypassing the curtain of misinformation draped over the issues by the congressional Democratic leadership, the White House, and too often, the media. They repeatedly shared their frustrations at hearing only one side of the budget debate.

And at each stop, they asked, "why can't you reach a compromise with the President on a balanced budget?"

The President's latest budget plan—the first plan of his that actually balances in 7 years—is similar to the four other budget plans he sent to Capitol Hill in the last year which, by the way, got no votes in the House and Senate. Throughout these weeks and weeks of budget negotiations, he has given up very little while Republicans have moved dramatically to help spur an agreement.

The President's budget cuts around the edges, but does not reform a thing. And I think we can say in one word the President's budget is a sham.

It does not reverse the kind of wild overspending that will continue to drag this Nation deeper into debt.

Spending remains unchecked under his latest plan, and $1 out of every $6 the President claims in deficit reduction comes not from cuts in spending, but from raising new revenue, new taxes.

It does not save Medicare and provide the choices for seniors our plan offers. Under the Clinton plan, Medicare remains a relic from 1960s that no longer works in the 1990s.

His budget does not reform Medicaid, either. We say let the States run Medicaid, and they will do a better job. The President's plan says, again, Washington has all the answers.

He does not offer meaningful tax relief. His tax cuts amount to only token tax relief, and with $66 billion in new taxes, the President's budget does nothing to reduce the tax liability of the country. His version of the $500 per-child tax credit is slowly phased in and then eliminated in 2002, and applies only to children 12 years old and younger.

He does not make fundamental changes in welfare to control spending.

In fact, his welfare proposals spend $20 billlon more than the bipartisan welfare bill passed by Congress. The President does not "end welfare as we know it," he extends welfare as we know it.

In reality, the President's budget plan is just a Band-Aid on a wound that is demanding emergency surgery. Yank off the Band-Aid after 7 years and the wound will not be healed, it will have festered and grown.

Mr. President, it will do no good to balance the budget in 2002 if it all unravels in 2003. And without a solid framework to work from, that is precisely where we would be heading under the President's version of a balanced budget.

That is how the freshman class answered the question each time we were asked why we have not been able to reach a budget compromise. We will not compromise our principles. No budget is better than a bad budget.

The President is right when he says the debate over the Federal budget is no longer just about dollars. It is about dollars and about something far more important: the future direction of this Nation, and which governing philosophy ought to lead us there.

The President says maybe we should wait until the next election and let the people decide what direction they want their Government to take. But the tax payers we met with in Knoxville, and Philadelphia, and Minneapolis, and Tulsa last week told us that is the change they thought they voted for in November 1994, when they turned this Government around by electing a new majority in Congress.

You know, President Clinton is going to come here to the Capitol tonight to deliver what will undoubtedly be a passionate speech on the State of the Union.

As we all know, he can be an impressive speaker. He will speak fervently and forcefully and, with any luck, he will wrap up in time for Sunday's Super Bowl kickoff.

I hope that what we hear tonight is a message of leadership, an acknowledgement of the awesome responsibility with which a President is entrusted, and a willingness to put aside a narrow political agenda in order to do what is best for the American people.

Only great leadership will lead this Nation toward the great days that await us.

What I am afraid we will get instead is a campaign event—the great kick-off to Bill Clinton's 1996 re-election campaign.

Judging by the folks we met around the country last week, he may have a tougher go of it than he thinks in the weeks and months ahead because at every stop on our freshman tour, Americans offered us their full support.

"Do not back down," "Hold the line," they said. "Get the budget balanced, but do it right." A lot of people told us they would be willing to wait a year for a responsible budget agreement, if that is what it takes.

Maybe then, they said, somebody a little more serious about balancing the budget will be occupying the Oval Office.

And so the revolution of 1994 continues, Mr. President.

That is the strong message my freshman colleagues and I bring with us back to Washington. And for our colleagues who may not have ventured beyond the confines of the Beltway recently, that is the message the American people are demanding we do not forget.

THE MYTH ABOUT PUBLIC SERVANTS[3]
DANIEL P. BEARD

*Commissioner, U.S. Bureau of Reclamation, 1993–95; born, Belling-
ham, WA, 1943; B.A, Western Washington University, 1965; M.A. and
Ph.D., University of Washington, 1973; executive vice president, Freshman Beard, Inc., Washington, D.C.; staff director, Committee on Resources, U.S. House of Representatives, 1991–92.*

Editors' introduction: Reading from a prepared text, Commissioner Daniel P. Beard praised the virtues of public service in
his address, before 2,500 students, their families, and friends
attending the University of California commencement exercises
at Berkeley, May 22, 1995. When Representative George Miller
printed Beard's speech in the *Congressional Record* (June 29,
1995), he wrote: "I know the Commissioner to be an exemplary
public servant from his work as the Staff Director of the Water
and Power Subcommittee."

During 1995–1996, President Clinton's Democratic administration, and the Republican controlled Congress fought continu-
ously over the cost and function of the federal government. At
one point, when the conflicting parties could not compromise on
cutting the federal budget all but essential agencies of the federal
government were shut down. Criticism of the government also included career federal employees. Beard recalled that "there had
been considerable press critical of public employees; I took a
stand on a controversial issue and that's why my speech was
well-received."

Now retired and a lobbyist and consultant with Freshman
Beard, Inc., Washington, D.C., Beard informed the editors that,
in the address below he "was trying to be inspirational and upbeat
at the same time. It was the most difficult speech I ever gave because the audience wasn't really there to hear me." However,
Beard's strategy was to mix humor with his basic message which
was: "Public service shouldn't be denigrated; that we should hon-
or public servants, not criticize them. The students liked the hu-

[3]Delivered at the University of California, Berkeley, CA, on May 22, 1995 at
3:00 p.m.

mor and brevity. The parents liked the message. An added
benefit was the reaction from government employees; they really
liked it. The reason the speech was so well-received was it was
timely."

Daniel P. Beard's speech: I have a confession to make: I have
worked in government for more than two decades. Even more
scandalous, I am a political appointee who believes it is an honor
to work with career public servants.

I guess those are dangerous things to admit these days, given
the strong undercurrent of suspicion and mistrust surrounding
public service. But they are beliefs I have expressed throughout
my career—and they are especially important to emphasize now
that I am leaving government.

We seem to be awash in a steady media diet of supposed examples of government employees who have gone too far. Of power-
mad bureaucrats harassing private citizens or squeezing the life
out of small businesses and property owners.

For a growing number of critics, everything that government
does is viciously wrong, or at least hopelessly wrong-headed. According to them, we cannot rely on public servants to strike a fair
balance between the public good and economic security.

Most of the critics of government rely on a volatile mixture
of myth and innuendo to make their case. They ignore the amaz-
ing contributions that millions of government workers have made
to American prosperity, peace, happiness and yes, freedom.

How completely different is today's atmosphere from the beginning of this century, an era dominated by the first true Republican reformer, Teddy Roosevelt. Roosevelt believed most deeply
and passionately in the values of public service.

"The first duty of an American citizen," he once said, "is that
he should work in politics; the second is that he shall do that work
in a practical manner; and the third is that it shall be done in ac-
cord with the highest principles of honor and justice."

Roosevelt spent five years as a member of the U.S. Civil Service Commission, and as its leading reformer worked to dismantle
the spoils system and institute what we have today: a merit-based
civil service system.

Before we malign government workers, let's think about who
they really are. They are the people who led the rescue in Oklahoma City—not who caused it. They are the ones who are

charged with apprehending those suspected of being responsible. Every day, they make their contributions to society, ensuring our food is safe to eat, the water fit to drink, and the air clean enough to breathe, teaching our children to read and write, protecting our neighborhoods and our nation as a whole.

Public servants are not monsters, and they are not strangers. All of us know them—they are our neighbors, friends, parents, children.

They are not, as the National Rifle Association would have us believe, "jack-booted thugs" who thrive on intimidating law-abiding citizens.

They are there to serve. Yes, they should be held strictly accountable and be efficient. And yes, sometimes they will do things that annoy us.

Who wants to be given a parking ticket—until someone blocks us in or out by parking illegally. Who wants to be made to conform to strict environmental laws—until we want clean water and air. Who wants government at all—until we want well-maintained highways, first-class public universities, tremendous medical and scientific technology, incredible national security and so on.

Public servants should not be castigated for doing their jobs. Most do a job that we couldn't do without. They deserve our respect.

The highest reward for any work is not what you get for it, but what you become by it. It is the goal of most government workers that our country becomes better by their work.

We should and do have vigorous and honest debate about what our government should be involved in. But, we can have it without vilifying public servants.

To all our nation's public servants, I say "thank you." You do a great deal of good for this country and the world—much, much more than many now give you credit for.

THE UNITED NATIONS AT FIFTY[4]
MADELEINE ALBRIGHT

U.S. Ambassador to United Nations; born Prague, Czechoslovakia, 1938; A.B. and Ph.D., Columbia University; staff of National Security Council; earlier a professor at Georgetown University.

Editors' introduction: In a speech in San Francisco, California, June 26, 1995, marking the 50th anniversary of the United Nations, the American Ambassador to the U.N., Madeleine Albright, asked citizens "to reject outright the forces of faction and fear that divide us, and . . . celebrate our diverse cultures and histories without denying the common humanity that binds us" (Cable News Network). When more than 140 leaders from around the world convened in New York for a three-day commemoration of the anniversary, many acknowledged both a need for reform and a need for renewed commitment by member nations to the "beleaguered organization." Among those attending were President Clinton, Boris Yeltsin, Fidel Castro, and Yasir Arafat. With the U.S. more than one billion dollars behind in its payments to the U.N., U.S. Representative Gerald B. H. Solomon complained that the international organization "has been spending money more carelessly than even the spendthrift Democratic Congresses of the past forty years" (*Congressional Record*, Nov. 1, 1995).

On November 8, 1995, the Congressional Human Rights Caucus, co-chaired by U.S. Representatives Tom Lantos (D, California) and John Porter (R, Illinois) sponsored a Congressional celebration of the 50th anniversary of the U.N. The occasion included a reception honoring Dr. Boutros Boutros-Ghali, Secretary General of the U.N., and U.S. Ambassador Madeleine Albright, a member of President Clinton's Cabinet. Colleagues from the House and Senate also participated. Geraldine Baum (*Los Angeles Times*, Feb. 8, 1995) wrote of the Ambassador: "At 57, Albright has had a full life—a childhood during which she fled Czechoslovakia not once but twice . . . and a career that went far beyond her expectations to where few women have gone

[4]Delivered in Washington, D.C., on November 8, 1995.

before. She pushes her own principles forcefully in private but speaks for the group in public as its unified voice. Albright is a savvy politician and will alter her vocabulary accordingly." Rather than read from a manuscript at the Congressional reception, Albright relied upon a few "talking points." In publishing this more impromptu talk in the *Congressional Record* (Nov. 8, 1995), Lantos observed: "As a result of the existence of the U.N., the world is now a better place than it would be otherwise. . . . The U.N. is in need of serious review and reform. . . . In our zeal for reform, . . . we [should] not lose sight of the vitally important role which the U.N. has played during the past half century."

Madeleine Albright's speech: Good evening fellow multilateralists.

Now, to some, multilateralism is a sin; sort of like watching PBS or liking art. And it is true that multilateralism is a terrible word; it has too many syllables; there's a little Latin in there; and it ends in i-s-m.

But supposedly, the big rivalry these days is between unilateralists and multilateralists. This is a phony debate. I have been studying, teaching and practicing foreign policy for more than 30 years, and I have yet to come across anyone who has accomplished anything without understanding that there will be times we have to act alone, and times when we can act with others at less cost and risk, and greater effectiveness.

That isn't unilateralism or multilateralism—it's realism.

On the things that matter most to our families, from drugs to terrorists to pollution to controlling our borders to creating new jobs, international cooperation isn't just an option, it is a necessity. And the UN is a unique mechanism for providing that cooperation.

This is the UN's 50th anniversary; but reading the newspapers, you would think, at times, we were observing not a birthday, but a wake.

We have such short memories. The UN at 50 is far stronger, effective and relevant than the UN of 40, 30, [20] or 10 years ago. Cold War divisions are gone; north-south differences have narrowed; the non-aligned movement is running out of factions to be non-aligned with.

Measured against impossible expectations, the UN will always fall short.

Measured in the difference it has made in people's lives, we can all take pride in what the UN has accomplished.

It matters that the ceasefire in Cyprus is holding; that confidence is being built in the Middle East; and that Namibia, Cambodia, Mozambique, El Salvador and Haiti have joined the great worldwide movement to democracy.

It matters that the economic pressure of sanctions has improved the climate for peace in the Balkans; penalized Libya for the terror of Pan Am 103; helped to consign apartheid to the dustbin of history; and forced Iraq to confess its program of deadly biological weapons.

It matters that millions of children each year live instead of die because they are immunized against childhood disease.

It matters that smallpox has been eradicated, that polio is on the way out, and that a global campaign to increase awareness about AIDS has been launched.

It matters that so many families in Somalia, Bosnia, Liberia, Sudan, the Caucasus, Afghanistan, Central America, and Southeast Asia owe their survival to the World Food Program and the UN High Commissioner for Refugees.

It matters that the IAEA is working to prevent the spread of nuclear weapons across the face of the earth.

And it matters that the War Crimes Tribunals for Rwanda and former Yugoslavia will strive to hold the perpetrators of ethnic cleansing and mass rape accountable for their crimes.

Let us never forget that the United Nations emerged not from a dream, but a nightmare. In the 1920's and 30's, the world squandered an opportunity to organize the peace. The result was the invasion of Manchuria, the conquest of Ethiopia, the betrayal of Munich, the depravity of the Holocaust and the devastation of world war.

This month, we observe the 50th anniversary of the start of the Nuremburg trials. This same month, we observe the start of the first trial of the War Crimes Tribunal for former Yugoslavia. A cynic might say that we have learned nothing; changed nothing; and forgotten the meaning of "never again" again. We cannot exclude the possibility that the cynic is right. We cannot deny the damnable duality of human nature.

But we can choose not to desert the struggle; to see our reflection not in Goebbels and Mladic, but in Anne Frank, Nelson Mandela, Václav Havel, Aung San Suu Kyi and the people who founded and built the United Nations.

We can understand there will be limits on what we accomplish; without placing unnecessary limits on what we attempt.

We can believe that humans do have the ability to rise above the hatreds of the past and to live together in mutual respect and peace.

We can believe that justice matters, that compassion is good, that freedom is never safe, and that the capacity to work effectively with others is a sign not of weakness, but of wisdom and strength.

And we can recognize that the principles embodied in the UN Charter matter not because they are so easy to obtain, but because they are so terribly hard.

When Republican Senator Arthur Vandenberg returned to Washington from the Convention in San Francisco where the UN Charter was drafted, he was challenged by those who thought it too idealistic, even utopian. He replied that:

"You may tell me that I have but to scan the present world with realistic eyes in order to see the fine phrases (of the Charter) . . . reduced to a shambles. . . . I reply that the nearer right you may be . . . the greater is the need for the new pattern which promises . . . to stem these evil tides."

The Truman-Vandenberg generation understood that although the noble aspects of human nature had made the UN possible, it was the ignoble aspects that had made it necessary.

It is up to us in our time to do what they did in their time. To accept the responsibilities of leadership. To defend freedom. And to explode outwards the potential of institutions like the UN to keep peace, extend law, promote progress and amplify respect for the dignity and value of every human being.

In that effort, I ask your help.

III. THE ENVIRONMENT

TO PROTECT THE *WHOLE* OF CREATION[1]
BRUCE BABBITT

United States Secretary of the Interior; born Los Angeles, CA, 1938; B.A,. Notre Dame, 1960; M.S., Newcastle, England, 1962; LL.B., Harvard Law School; Governor of Arizona, 1978–87; Attorney General of Arizona, 1975–78; Thomas Jefferson Award, National Wildlife Federation, 1981.

Editors' introduction: By June 27, 1995, conservative Democrat and Republican U.S. Senators opposed the existing "requirement that manufacturers disclose how much they pollute." On July 16, 1995, Republicans backed fewer restrictions on "mining, grazing, logging, toxic wastes, water quality, endangered species, and pesticides" (John H. Cushman, *New York Times*, June 28 & July 17, 1995). Concerned that proposed legislation by conservatives threatened the 1973 Endangered Species Act, which was up for renewal, the Evangelical Environmental Network mailed "*Let the Earth Be Glad* kits to 33,000 evangelical churches. About 1,000 churches responded to the call to become *'Noah Congregations'*." Calvin B. DeWitt, 60, one of the founders of the Network, stated, "Only the Creator has a right to destroy His creation" (*Washington Post*, February 17, 1996). Having failed to defeat a resolution in the U.S. Senate that would "make it much easier for oil companies to destroy our . . . Arctic National Wildlife Refuge in Alaska," in a speech to the annual meeting of Project Managers, U.S. Fish and Wildlife Service, in Atlanta, May 25, 1995, Brock Evans, Vice President for National Issues of The National Audubon Society, warned that "these are scary, intense, and very dangerous times for . . . environmentalists who love our American public lands" (*Vital Speeches*, Sept. 1, 1995). Aware of mounting "support for strong environmental protection," President Clinton took a more combative stance on

[1]Delivered at the Campion Renewal Center, Weston, MA, on November 11, 1995.

behalf of environmental laws. On February 11, 1996, a Presidential panel with adversaries from both sides recommended "giv[ing] businesses more flexibility in preventing pollution—but only if they can perform better than is required under the current system of strict safeguards" (Cushman, *New York Times*, July 5, 1995 & Feb. 12, 1996).

"After a year's battering . . . by the Republican Congress on natural resources issues, while plant[ing] Oregon grapes . . . on the banks of Fanno Creek," on November 11, 1995, Bruce Babbitt, U.S. Secretary of the Interior, defended the nation's environment and the laws that protected it. In this address, entitled "'Between the Flood and the Rainbow,' Our Covenant: To Protect the *Whole* of Creation," Babbitt addressed a joint meeting of the National Religious Partnership for the Environment, and the American Association for the Advancement of Science. Drawing upon the initiatives of John Muir and Rachel Carson, Babbitt underscored "the link between spirituality and preserving the environment" (*Oregonian*, March 1, 1996). Babbitt spoke in the late morning to an audience of 500 scientists and theologians from around the United States meeting at the Campion Renewal Center, Weston, MA, near Boston. He explained to the editors of this volume that his purpose was to "find a values basis for the U.S.A. beyond what is good for humans." To reach that end, using notes and some memorized thoughts, he employed "personal testimony and inquir[ed] into the values that underlie our law." Babbitt found response to his speech to be "overwhelmingly positive; the only negatives, were from the extreme right who take words out of context." Representative Helen Chenoweth opposed Babbitt's linking of environmental causes with religion in a speech also contained in this volume. Chenoweth said Babbitt's address "caused quite a shakeup among religious groups and environmentalists alike." A letter from the Interfaith Impact Foundation stated that Babbitt's speech addressed "the essential role played by faith communities in defending the environment," and invited him to "give the plenary address on ecology" at their meeting in Washington, D.C., March 3-6, 1996.

Bruce Babbitt's speech: A wolf's green eyes, a sacred blue mountain, the words from Genesis, and the answers of children all reveal the religious values manifest in the 1973 Endangered Species Act.

I began 1995 with one of the more memorable events of my lifetime. It took place in the heart of Yellowstone National Park, during the first week of January, a time when a layer of deep, pure snow blanketed the first protected landscape in America. But for all it's beauty, over the past 60 years this landscape had been an incomplete ecosystem; by the 1930s, government-paid hunters had systematically eradicated the predator at the top of the food chain: the American grey wolf.

I was there on that day, knee deep in the snow, because I had been given the honor of carrying the first wolves back into that landscape. Through the work of conservation laws, I was there to restore the natural cycle, to make Yellowstone complete.

The first wolf was an Alpha female, and after I set her down in the transition area, where she would later mate and bear wild pups, I looked through the grate into the green eyes of this magnificent creature, within this spectacular landscape, and was profoundly moved by the elevating nature of America's conservation laws: laws with the power to make creation whole.

I then returned to Washington, where a new Congress was being sworn into office, and witnessed power of a different kind.

First I witnessed an attack on our national lands, an all-out attempt to abolish our American tradition of public places—whether national parks, forests, historic sites, wildlife refuges, and recreation areas. Look quickly about you, name your favorite place: a beach in New York harbor; the Appomattox Courthouse; the great western ski areas; the caribou refuge in the Arctic; or the pristine waters off the Florida Keys. For each of these places is at risk. Last month in the Denver *Post*, the Chairman of the House Subcommittee on Public Lands estimated that his committee may have to close more than 100 of the Park Service's 369 units. In these times, it seems that no part of our history or our natural heritage is sufficiently important to protect and preserve for the benefit of all Americans.

Next I witnessed an attack that targets the 1972 Clean Water Act, the most successful of all our enviromental laws. Until that Act passed, slaughterhouses, pulp mills and factories from Boise to Boston to Baton Rouge spewed raw waste into our waterfronts. Yet 23 years later, as I visited America's cities, I saw that Act restoring those rivers, breathing new life into once-dead waters. I saw people gather on clean banks to fish, sail, swim, eat and live. I saw that, as the Act helps cities restore our waters, those waters restore our cities themselves. And then I saw Congress rushing to tear that Act apart.

But finally, more than any of our environmental laws, the Act they have most aggressively singled out for elimination—one that made Yellowstone complete—is the 1973 Endangered Species Act.

Never mind that this Act is working, having saved 99 percent of all listed species; never mind that it effectively protects hundreds of plants and animals, from grizzly bears to whooping cranes to greenback cutthroat trout; never mind that it is doing so while costing each American 16 cents per year.

For the new Congress—while allowing for the above charismatic species, plus a dozen other species good for hunting and fishing, plus, just for good measure, the bald eagle—can find absolutely no reason to protect all species in general.

Who cares, they ask, if the spotted owl goes extinct? We won't miss it, or, for that matter, the Texas blind salamander or the kangaroo rat. And that goes double for the fairy shrimp, the burying beetle, the Delphi sands flower-loving fly and the virgin spine dace! If they get in our way, if humans drive some creatures to extinction, well, that's just too bad.

Over the past year that is, I think, a fairly accurate summary of how the new majority in Congress has expressed its opinion of the Endangered Species Act.

They are not, however, the only Americans who have expressed an opinion on this issue.

Recently I read an account of a Los Angeles "Eco-Expos" last April, where children were invited to write down their answers to the basic question: "Why save endangered species?"

One child, Gabriel, answered, "Because God gave us the animals."

Travis and Gina wrote, "Because we love them."

A third answered, "Because we'll be lonely without them."

Still another wrote, "Because they're a part of our life. If we didn't have them, it would not be a complete world. The Lord put them on earth to be enjoyed, not destroyed."

Now, in my lifetime I have heard many, many political, agricultural, scientific, medical and ecological reasons for saving endangered species. I have in fact hired biologists and ecologists for just that purpose. All their reasons have to do with providing humans with potential cures for disease, or yielding humans new strains of drought-resistant crops, or offering humans bioremediation of oil spills, or thousands of other justifications of why species are useful to humans.

But none of their reasons moved me like the children's.

For these children are speaking and writing in plain words a complex notion that has either been lost, or forgotten, or never learned by some members of Congress, and indeed by many of us.

The children are expressing the moral and spiritual imperative that there may be a higher purpose inherent in creation, demanding our respect and our stewardship quite apart from whether a particular species is or ever will be of material use to mankind. They see in creation what our adult political leaders refuse to acknowledge. They express an answer that can be reduced to one word: values.

I remember when I was their age, a child growing up in a small town in Northern Arizona. I learned my religious values through the Catholic Church, which, in that era, in that Judeo-Christian tradition, kept silent on our moral obligation to nature. By its silence the church implicitly sanctioned the prevailing view of the earth as something to be used and disposed however we saw fit, without any higher obligation. In all the years that I attended Sunday mass, hearing hundreds of homilies and sermons, there was never any reference, any link, to our natural heritage or to the spiritual meaning of the land surrounding us.

Yet, outside that church I always had a nagging instinct that the vast landscape *was* somehow sacred, and holy, and connected to me in a sense that my catechism ignored.

At the edge of my home town a great blue mountain called the San Francisco Peaks soars up out of the desert to a snowy summit, snagging clouds on its crest, changing color with the seasons. It was always a mystical, evocative presence in our daily lives. To me that mountain, named by Spanish missionaries for Saint Francis, remains a manifestation of the presence of our Creator.

That I was not alone in this view was something I had to discover through a very different religion. For on the opposite side of the blue mountain, in small pueblos on the high mesas that stretch away toward the north, lived the Hopi Indians. And it was a young Hopi friend who taught me that the blue mountain was, truly, a sacred place.

One Sunday morning in June he led me out to the mesa top villages where I watched as the Kachina filed into the plaza, arriving from the snowy heights of the mountain, bringing blessings from another world.

Another time he took me to the ceremonials where the priests of the snake clan chanted for rain and then released live rattlesnakes to carry their prayers to the spirits deep within the earth.

Later I went with him to a bubbling spring, deep in the Grand Canyon, lined with pahoes—the prayer feathers—where his ancestors had emerged from another world to populate this earth.

By the end of that summer I came to believe, deeply and irrevocably, that the land, and that blue mountain, and all the plants and animals in the natural world are together a direct reflection of divinity, that creation is a plan of God, and I saw, in the words of Emerson, "the visible as proceeding from the invisible."

That awakening made me acutely aware of a vacancy, a poverty amidst my own rich religious tradition. I felt I had to either embrace a borrowed culture, or turn back and have a second look at my own. And while priests then, as now, are not too fond of people rummaging about in the Bible to draw our own meanings, I chose the latter, asking: Is there nothing in our Western, Judeo-Christian tradition that speaks to our natural heritage and the sacredness of that blue mountain? Is there nothing that can connect me to the surrounding Creation?

There are those who argue that there isn't.

There are those industrial apologists who, when asked about Judeo-Christian values relating to the environment, reply that the material world, including the environment, is just an incidental fact, of no significance in the relation between us and our Creator.

They cite the first verses of Genesis, concluding that God gave Adam and his descendants the absolute, unqualified right to "subdue" the earth and gave man "dominion over the fish of the sea, and over the fowl of the air, and over every living thing that moveth upon the earth." God, they assert, put the earth here for the disposal of man in whatever manner he sees fit. Period.

They should read a few verses further.

For there, in the account of the Deluge, the Bible conveys a far different message about our relation to God and to the earth. In Genesis, Noah was commanded to take into the ark two by two and seven by seven every living thing in creation, the clean and the unclean.

He did not specify that Noah should limit the ark to two charismatic species, two good for hunting, two species that might provide some cure down the road, and, say, two that draw crowds to the city zoo.

No, He specified *the whole of creation*. And when the waters receded, and the dove flew off to dry land, God set all the creatures free, commanding them to multiply upon the earth.

Then, in the words of the covenant with Noah, "when the rainbow appears in the clouds, I will see it and remember the everlasting covenant between me and all living things on earth."

Thus we are instructed that this everlasting covenant was made to protect the whole of creation, not for the exclusive use and disposition of mankind, but for the purposes of the Creator.

Now, we all know that the commandment to protect creation in all its diversity does not come to us with detailed operating instructions. It is left to us to translate a moral imperative into a way of life and into public policy. Which we did. Compelled by this ancient command, modern America turned to the national legislature which forged our collective moral imperative into one landmark law: the 1973 Endangered Species Act.

The trouble is that during the first twenty years of the Endangered Species Act scientists and administrators and other well-intentioned people somehow lost sight of that value—to protect the *whole* of creation—and instead took a fragmented, mechanistic approach to preserve individual species. Isolated specialists working in secluded regions waited until the eleventh hour to act, then heroically rescued species—one at a time.

Sometimes the result was dramatic recovery, but often the result was chaos, conflict, and continuing long term decline. In the Pacific Northwest, for example, the spotted owl was listed even as federal agencies went forward with clear cutting. Efforts to save the alligator proceeded even as the Everglades shrivelled from diverted waters. They listed California salmon runs even as water users continued to deplete the spawning streams.

It is only in the last few years that have we recovered, like a lost lens, our ancient religious values. This lens lets us see not human-drawn distinctions—as if creation could ever be compartmentalized into a million discrete parts, each living in relative isolation from the others—but rather the interwoven wholeness of creation.

Not surprisingly, when we can see past these man-made divisions, the work of protecting God's creation grows both easier and clearer.

It unites all state, county and federal workers under a common moral goal. It erases artificial borders so we can see the full range of a natural habitat, whether wetland, forest, stream or desert expanse. And it makes us see all the creatures that are collectively rooted to one habitat, and how, by keeping that habitat whole and intact, we ensure the survival of the species.

For example, in the Cascades, the spotted owl's decline was only part of the collapsing habitat of the ancient forests. When seen as a whole, that habitat stretched from Canada to San Francisco. Not one but thousands of species, from waterfowl of the air to the salmon in their streams, depended for their survival on the unique rain forest amidst Douglas fir, hemlock and red cedar.

Our response was the President's Forest plan, a holistic regional agreement forged with state and local officials and the private sector. Across three state borders, it keeps critical habitat intact, provides buffer zones along salmon streams and coastal areas, and elsewhere provides a sustainable timber harvest for generations to come.

That's also the lesson of Everglades National Park, where great flocks of wading birds are declining because their shallow feeding waters were drying up and dying off. Only by erasing park bourndaries could we trace the problem to its source, hundreds of miles upstream, where agriculture and cities were diverting the shallow water for their own needs. Only by looking at the whole South Florida watershed, could state and federal agencies unite to put the parts back together, restore the severed estuaries, revive the Park, and satisfy the needs of farmers, fishermen, ecologists and water users from Miami to Orlando.

This holistic approach is working to protect creation in the most fragmented habitats of America: from salmon runs in California's Central Valley to the red-cockaded woodpecker across Southeastern hardwood forests; from the Sand Hill Cranes on the headwaters of the Platte River in Central Nebraska to the desert tortoise of the Mojave Reserve. I'd like to say that the possibilities are limited only by our imagination and our commitment to honor the instructions of Genesis.

But more and more, the possibilities are also limited by some members of Congress. Whenever I confront some of these bills that are routinely introduced, bills sometimes openly written by industrial lobbyists, bills that systematically eviscerate the Endangered Species Act, I take refuge and inspiration from the simple written answers of those children at the Los Angeles expo.

But I sometimes wonder if children are the only ones who express religious values when talking about endangered species. I wonder if anyone else in America is trying to restore an ounce of humility to mankind, reminding our political leaders that the earth is a sacred precinct, designed by and for the purposes of the Creator.

I got my answer last month.

I read letter after letter from five different religious orders, representing tens of millions of chuchgoers, all opposing a House bill to weaken the Endangered Species Act. They opposed it not for technical or scientific or agricultural or medical reasons, but for spiritual reasons.

And I was moved not only by how such diverse faiths could reach so pure an agreement against this bill, but by the common language and terms with which they opposed it, language that echoed the voices of the children:

One letter, from the Presbyterian Church, said: "Contemporary moral issues are related to our understanding of nature and humanity's place in them." The Reform Hebrew Congregation wrote: "Our tradition teaches us that the earth and all of its creatures are the work and the possessions of the Creator." And the Mennonite Church wrote: "We need to hear and obey the command of our Creator who instructed us to be stewards of God's creation."

And suddenly, at that moment, I understood exactly why some members of Congress react with such unrestrained fear and loathing towards the Endangered Species Act. I understood why they tried to ban all those letters from the *Congressional Record*. I understood why they are so deeply disturbed by the prospect of religious values entering the national debate.

For if they heard that command of our Creator, if they truly listened to His instructions to be responsible stewards, then their entire framework of human rationalizations for tearing apart the Act comes to nought.

I conclude here tonight by affirming that those religious values remain at the heart of the Endangered Species Act, that they make themselves manifest through the green eyes of the grey wolf, through the call of the whooping crane, through the splash of the Pacific salmon, through the voices of America's children.

We are living between the flood and the rainbow: between the threats to creation on the one side and God's covenant to protect life on the other.

Why should we save endangered species?

Let us answer this question with one voice, the voice of the child at that expo, who scrawled her answer at the very bottom of the sheet:

"Because we can."

PRESERVING THE ENVIRONMENT AND LIBERTY[2]
HELEN CHENOWETH

Republican Member of U.S. House of Representatives from Idaho; born eastern Kansas; attended Whitworth College, Spokane, WA; medical and legal management consultant, 1964–75; Congressional subcommittees: Energy and Mineral Resources, Water and Power Resources, Research Conservation, Research and Forestry.

Editors' introduction: In Bruce Babbitt's speech entitled "Our Covenant: To Protect the *Whole* of Creation," also in this volume, the U.S. Interior Secretary maintained that, "when we can see past . . . man-made divisions, the work of protecting God's creation grows both easier and clearer." In a speech on January 31, 1996, entitled "Preserving the Environment and Liberty," Representative Helen Chenoweth responded to Babbitt's argument in a special orders address. Chenoweth related to the editors of this volume that her purpose in the speech below was "to draw public attention to the growing connection between religion and the federal government's environmental policy." Chenoweth quoted from Babbitt's speech to "demonstrate the secretary's view of environmentalism as a religion"; she offered "examples of how over-zealous environmental regulations are

[2]Delivered at the United States House of Representatives, Washington, D.C., on January 31, 1996.

negatively impacting Idaho." Chenoweth contended that "environmentalism need not be a religion, especially for the purpose of setting government policy. Science and logic . . . should be the driving forces behind laws passed to protect the environment."

Using notes, Chenoweth spoke in the late afternoon to between fifteen and twenty persons on the floor of the U.S. House, and to a national television audience. Chenoweth's address came "the same day that a group of religious conservatives, citing key passages of the Bible, launched a campaign to protect and strengthen the existing Endangered Species Act" ((AP) *Idaho Press-Tribune*, Feb. 3, 1996). Chenoweth reported that "calls from the general public to her office were mostly in agreement with her speech; some environmental groups made negative comments in the press." Chenoweth opposed reintroducing wolves into Idaho. While not advocating reintroducing the wolves, Republican Governor Phil Batt said, "Maybe there's a case for that." According to the *Washington Post* (Al Kamen, Feb. 5, 1996), some Republicans believe that although "their drive to change the nation's environmental laws is costing them, . . . Chenoweth is not about to abandon her principles for a few lousy votes."

Helen Chenoweth's speech: Mr. Speaker, it is a rare individual who does not want an effective environmental policy. Sometimes these policies, or the remedies thereof, have been called extreme, just like we heard from my friends on the other side of the aisle. I am one of the freshman Members, but I find it interesting that a party who has lost its vision can use only one word to define the other party, and that is the word "extreme." I beg of my colleagues on the other side of the aisle to come up with alternative programs that will benefit the American people.

I just have to say Mr. Speaker, this was not a planned part of my speech, but I do want to say that it is private individuals who risk and who invest who employ Americans. I join the gentlewoman from Ohio [Ms. Kaptur], a woman I admire greatly, about the fact that we do want to keep American jobs here in America. I do agree with her there. But, you know, we either have one of two employers: Either you, the taxpayers, are employing individuals through government, or we have private businesses employing people. I prefer private entrepreneurs in employing people and downsizing government.

Mr. Speaker, it is a rare individual who doesn't want an effective environmental policy. We all want to promote the wise use of America's natural resources, but the driving force behind our current policies have little to do with sound science, foresight, or reason. Instead, environmental policies are driven by a kind of emotional spiritualism that threatens the very foundation of our society, by eroding basic principles of our Constitution.

Mr. Speaker, if there is one quote I could center my remarks around today, I think it would be a personal statement made by Thomas Jefferson, who probably was the world's greatest articulator of man's heavenly endowed individual rights and liberties. Jefferson wrote in 1776:

I may grow rich by an art I am compelled to follow, I may recover health by medicines I am compelled to take against my own judgment; but I cannot be saved by a worship I disbelieve and abhor.

Mr. Speaker, the very first clause of the very first amendment to our Constitution states that "Congress shall make no law respecting an establishment of religion," and yet there is increasing evidence of a government sponsored religion in America. This religion, a cloudy mixture of new age mysticism, Native American folklore, and primitive Earth worship, (Pantheism) is being promoted and enforced by the Clinton administration in violation of our rights and freedoms.

Proponents of this new-environmentalism are the first to recognize its religious nature. Just to name a few: Sierra Club Director David Brower announced "We are a kind of religion." Scientist James Lovelock, author of the bestseller "Gaia," admits that "Gaia is a religious as well as a scientific concept." Bill McKibbon, author of "The End of Nature," proclaimed that "it is not in God's house that I feel his presence most—it is in His outdoors." According to columnist Alston Chase, nearly all environmental leaders have conceded that environmentalism is a religious movement.

The trouble is that these sentiments are not just expressed by leaders in the environmental movement, but frequently, by government leaders who influence and promulgate the regulations we live under. When Vice President AL GORE was invited to speak at the Episcopal Cathedral of St. John the Divine, he sermonized that "God is not separate from the Earth." Espousal of this environmental religion by political leaders and regulators carries profound constitutional implications.

I recently came across the transcript of a speech delivered by U.S. Secretary of the Interior Bruce Babbitt on November 11 to a joint meeting of the National Religious Partnership for the Environment and the American Association for the Advancement of Science. It was entitled "Between the flood and the rainbow: Our Covenant to Protect the Whole of Creation." In this speech, Babbitt explains how he became disillusioned with Christianity because the commandment that man should have dominion "over every living thing that moveth upon the Earth" conflicted with his view of nature's supremacy. "I always had a nagging instinct," he explained, "that the vast landscape was somehow sacred, and holy, and connected to me in a sense that my catechism ignored." Babbitt explains how a young Hopi friend taught him "that the blue mountain was, truly, a sacred place," and he became "acutely aware of a vacancy, a poverty amidst [his] own religious tradition."

To fill this vacancy he adopted the new environmentalism, and he has every intention of regulating and enforcing his dream of utopia into reality.

You may ask, what is the harm of public officials maintaining deeply held beliefs? The problem, Mr. Speaker comes when those deeply held beliefs become the driving force for policy which that nonbelievers face persecution. Mr. Babbitt has made it clear that environmentalism—the religion—is driving this Nation's regulatory scheme. This is a violation of the establishment clause of the Constitution. Its mothers our values and it threatens our liberties.

James Madison wrote his great "Memorial and Remonstrance" against a Virginia tax for the support of an established church. In it, he eloquently argued that a true religion did not need the support of law; that no person, either believer or nonbeliever, should be taxed to support a religious institution of any kind; that the best interest of a society required that the minds of men always be wholly free; and that cruel persecution were the inevitable result of government-established religions.

Madison was right. The backbone of America—workers, small businessmen, and property owners—are becoming victims of this new-environmentalism.

Businesses like Stibnite Mine in my district, whose mining operation was shut down for 2 years waiting for the National Marine Fisheries Service to determine whether they could haul supplies on a Forest Service road.

People like the Yantis family in my district, who were told by the National Marine Fisheries Service that they should just give up their right to irrigate for a fish that is not instream now, but could be one day.

People like a Minnesota farmer who had two 1-acre glacial potholes on his property. To make farming around them easier, the farmer filled one and expanded the other two acres. The U.S. Army Corps of Engineers objected, and the Federal Government ordered him to dig out the pothole he had filled and fined him $45,000.

Whole families throughout the Northwest who have lost their jobs because government restrictions and environmental lawsuits have shut down the region's ability to keep forests healthy.

Farmers in the Bruneau Valley whose livelihoods have been held hostage to a snail the size of a buck shot. The Fish and Wildlife Service has yet to scientifically prove that farming activities have an effect on the snail.

For those who still refuse to see the dangerous character of an established religious environmental movement, let me give you another example:

Wayne and Jean Hage bought a cattle ranch in Nevada in 1978. The former owner had been forced to sell because the regulatory pressure by the U.S. Forest Service had become unbearable. But Hage was confident that he could work with the Forest Service to resolve any problems that might occur. He was wrong. Problems started when, without warning or notification, a nearby Forest Service Ranger Station began to pump water from a critical spring on Hage's property into the ranger's cabin. The Forest Service maintained a fence around the spring so that cattle could not drink, but, Hage felt that if the Service needed the water an amicable agreement could be reached. The Forest Service refused to cooperate, and when Hage held a field hearing on the issue, they launched an all-out holy-war against the rancher.

For the sacrilege of questioning Forest Service actions, Wayne was contacted no less than 110 times with violations of bureaucratic regulations. Most, if not all, were wild goose chases, but each required time consuming and often expensive responses. The Forest Service even resorted to several armed raids on the ranch, confiscating 104 head of cattle and keeping the proceeds of their sale. Hage also faced felony charges for clearing brush from his own irrigation drains. The charges were thrown out by the courts, but this was the last straw—Hage filed a suit for the regulatory and physical taking of his ranch.

Unfortunately, CIGNA Corporation, the lender and lien holder on Hage's property is one of the environmentalist faithful, and has been attempting to foreclose on the property to effectively kill the case. CIGNA is a major corporate donor to the National Wildlife Federation which is acting as a friend of the court on behalf of the Forest Service. This is an organization that instructs environmental activists on how to use Forest Service and Bureau of Land Management regulatory power to "Make it so expensive for the rancher to operate that he goes broke."

Mr. Speaker, there is something seriously wrong with this picture.

Environmentalism need not be a religion. It could—and should—be based on science and logic and aimed at secular goals. But Secretary Babbitt rejects the protection of species for potential cures for disease, or new strains of drought-resistant crops, or bioremediation of oil spills, in favor of uniting "all state, county and federal workers under a common moral goal." He concluded his speech by affirming that "religious values remain at the heart of the Endangered Species Act, that they make themselves manifest through the green eyes of the grey wolf, through the call of the whooping crane, through the splash of the Pacific salmon."

The fact that this moral philosophy makes villains of hard working, productive citizens makes it repugnant to American values. The fact that it dismisses science prevents technological progress. The fact that it violates the Establishment Clause of the Constitution makes it an attack on our form of government. And the fact that it places obstacles in the way of American prosperity makes it a threat to our children's future.

Mr. Speaker, policies inspired by this new green religion are having devastating effects on my State. One example that I think exemplifies this new trend is unnecessary introduction of predators such as wolves and grizzlies against the will of the people and at great expense to the taxpayer.

Many people do not realize that the idea of releasing wolves in Idaho and in the west is not a new one. There were attempts as far back as 1982, when Senator CRAIG held the seat that I hold now. At that time, when the U.S. Fish and Wildlife Service introduced this idea, the plan was quickly shelved after then-Congressman CRAIG held hearings in which obvious flaws of artificially introducing the wolves were exposed.

In those hearings biologists admitted that the wolf was recovering naturally in Canada and Alaska, where there are currently as many as 40,000 to 50,000 of the grey wolves. Moreover, the plan was soundly rejected after it became clear what the consequences would be of introducing a dangerous predator into an area that was no longer completely wild, but in fact, where there are activities such as ranching, logging, mining, and recreation.

The mere suggestion of introducing wolves prompted the State legislature to pass a number of bills prohibiting the introduction of wolves unless it was under the terms and conditions of the State. I would like to insert into the *Record* the testimony of State representative JoAn Wood, who came before the House Resources Committee and testified to the long history of Idaho's objection to Federal wolf introductions.

Nevertheless, when President Clinton was elected, Bruce Babbitt, the President's appointed Secretary of the Interior, again resurrected the idea of introducing wolves in the West. This time, instead of trying to establish a sound, practical, scientific basis for the program, the Government promoted wolf introduction as a romantic notion of restoring the western ecosystem to its pre-Colombian state. Indeed, Mr. Babbitt has gone as far as saying that it fulfills a "spiritual" void. Mr. Babbitt proclaimed in his November 11 speech that wolf introduction efforts were driven by the "elevated nature of America's conservation laws: laws with the power to make creation whole. . . . " in essence recover "our ancient religious values."

The Department of the Interior also responded differently to the avid oppoition to wolf reintroduction by States of Montana, Idaho, and Wyoming. The Fish and Wildlife Service promised the States that no wolves would be released until an agreement of how these wolves would be managed was in place. The Department of the Interior, in conjunction with the many environmental groups also initiated a large scale nationwide advertising campaign—in places where nobody would have to worry about managing the critters—to sell the romantic notion of returning these animals to the west.

Very little has been mentioned during the governments publicly campaign blitz of the overall costs of the wolf introduction, which includes aircraft, ground vehicles, equipment such as kennels, shipping crates, sophisticated radar tracking devices, radio collars, tranquilizing guns, and extensive staff of biologists, veterinarians, technicians, and administrators—not to mention a massive publicity campaign. Added up, it amounts to about $1 million per wolf.

I first dealt with Mr. Babbitt's infatuation with the green eyes of the wolf just after I was sworn in to represent the citizens of Idaho's First Congressional District. It was apparent that after the fiscally austere Republicans won the majority in Congress, Babbitt determined that the release of the wolves must be greatly expedited or his chance "to make nature whole" would once again be jeopardized. We found that his attempts to work out an arrangement with the States were not only completely disingenuous, but merely used as a device to detour the legitimate concerns of the States while he found a way to implement his plan. When Babbitt realized that his costly wolf scheme could come under scrutiny by this Congress, he went into emergency mode, bypassing all the processes, including State laws and section 6(f) of the Endangered Species Act which specifically requires the Secretary to work in coordination with the States in any introduction effort. He did this while ignoring the pleas of Governors and legislators to not proceed, but by actually speeding up the capture of the wolves.

By early January, just days after the new Congress had been sworn in, Babbitt had his wolves ready to be released at Yellowstone and in Idaho. My office received a firestorm of pleas and concerns from constituents and State officials calling for an immediate halt to the releases. In fact, one of my first official acts as a Congressman was to send a letter to the Secretary requesting that he halt any releases, and at the very least let due process take place. Babbitt defiantly responded by immediately releasing the wolves into Idaho—and even forging a highly questionable agreement with the Nez Perce Indian Tribe to manage the wolves.

Despite all, Secretary Babbitt proceeded with the release of his imprisoned green-eyed friends—although I don't know how anyone can consider him a friend of the wolf considering the abrupt way these wolves were tracked down and shot by a tranquilizer gun, forced into a pen, had a collar placed around their neck, taken away from their native habitat, and released into unfamiliar and unfriendly territory. Moreover, problems resulting from the unnatural methods used became evident when wolves which were released into Yellowstone, that were under the care of humans for weeks, refused for a time to leave their newfound comforts and security. Even now the wolves, which in the wild steer clear of humans, are routinely seen—and quite possibly fed—by many of the tourists visiting the park. It is easy to see that the wolf program in Yellowstone Park has done nothing more than create more dependents on the Government dole.

The released wolves faced—and caused—even more dire consequences in Idaho. Shortly after the wolves were released in Central Idaho, a wolf was shot near Salmon after feeding on the carcass of a newborn calf. The body of the wolf was found on the property of a 74-year-old World War II veteran and rancher by the name of Mr. Gene Hussey. The reaction of the Fish and Wildlife Service was to initiate a fullblown investigation that included a $500,000 autopsy performed on the dead wolf. The Fish and Wildlife Service obtained a search warrant, and without notifying Mr. Hussey or the local sheriff, proceeded to send several officers to investigate Mr. Hussey's property. In a hearing about this incident held jointly with the Resources and Agriculture Committees, on which I sit, Mr. Hussey testified that on arriving home from his neighbor's house, he discovered several armed Fish and Wildlife officers crawling over his gate—damaging the gate in the process—and refusing to heed his warnings to leave his property until the local sheriff arrived. The predicament escalated to the point that the Federal agents accused this 74-year-old man of throwing rocks at them, and rushed across a stream to confront him about it. In the meantime, the local sheriff, Mr. Barsalou was speeding to the scene—very concerned about the possibility of a violent confrontation. Fortunately, he was able to arrive in time to defuse the situation.

After some of the problems that we have witnessed with the release of only 14 wolves last year, I am amazed to see the media reporting the program as "remarkably successful." I was even more disappointed to find out that even during the Government shutdown, and before their appropriations were approved, the Fish and Wildlife Service was busy preparing to capture another 30 wolves in Canada for release in Idaho and Wyoming. The Service has spared no expense and has let nothing stop them including inclement weather, lack of appropriations, animal rights protesters, the continued disapproval of the State legislature, and another call by this Congressman to refrain from capturing and releasing more wolves.

Apparently one of Mr. Babbitt's green-eyed friends did not like the whole idea and bit one of his handlers before receiving the unlucky fate of being killed by one of the Fish and Wildlife officials. Of course, if I had just been tracked down from my home, snared, darted, caged, drugged, and jostled, I would have bitten someone too.

The truth of the matter is that there remain many unanswered questions and unaddressed concerns about the wolf introduction program. Despite the fact that the Government continues to disregard the wishes of the local citizens, to implement a program that serves no scientific purpose, creates the potential for more conflicts, and costs taxpayers a bundle, the Government and the national media continue to paint the program as a better than expected success with few hitches. I believe this is because the media, like Mr. Babbitt, are not focusing on the logic or scientific merits of the program, but on how well it has fulfilled their own spiritual expectations.

Some wonder why I have fought so hard against a Federal program that has little direct impact on most Americans. I fight because I believe that we should be practicing great fiscal constraint, because excessive deficits threaten the future stability of this country. I fight because the taxpayer deserves to know that millions of their dollars are being spent on aircraft outfitted with sophisticated radio equipment which daily track a handful of confused wolves meandering about and stirring up trouble in the mountains of Idaho, Wyoming, and Montana.

I also fight because I believe there are deep implications about the wolf introduction program that affects all Americans—and that is the precedent it has set.

Now the Federal Government is finalizing plans to introduce an even more dangerous predator into the Selway-Bitteroot mountain range located in Idaho and Montana—the grizzly bear. Mr. Speaker, only a few years ago—the very idea of introducing grizzlies into central Idaho was considered pure lunacy. Why? Quite frankly, the grizzly bear, a species that now numbers over 100,000 in Canada, Alaska, parts of Montana, and in Yellowstone, simply has a propensity for violence against humans and animals. Last year there were numerous incidents of bear maulings during unprovoked situations. In one case a hiker was merely taking his shoes and socks off to cool his feet in a mountain stream when the odor of his socks apparently caught the attention of a nearby grizzly. And in the State of Wyoming and Montana, there has been an epidemic of nuisance bears which have been killing cattle and sheep, and rummaging around human habitation. Some are even suggesting that the grizzly no longer needs the special protection of the Endangered Species Act.

Mr. Speaker, the response that I have received from my constituents—even some who do not normally agree with me—has been overwhelmingly against the introduction of the grizzly. I believe that some in the forest industry have been driven by fear or strong coercive tactics into supporting a program that simply will not work. Other than that, the reaction against the idea comes from all types of individuals and for many legitimate reasons. Campers and hikers are concerned for obvious safety reasons, and that many of the trails and areas would be made off-limits. Hunters are concerned about dramatic reductions in game animal population. Ranchers are concerned about the loss of cattle and road closures. Miners are concerned about the possibility of restrictions on their activity as well, and property owners are deeply concerned about bears foraging about their garbage, and around their homes. Overall, people are not only afraid of the potential danger of having the bears in their backyard, but also having severe restrictions in accessing the forests and lands, both for recreational and industrial purposes. In fact the public comments compiled by the Fish and Wildlife Service show overwhelming opposition to the grizzly introduction plan in the Selway-Bitteroot coming from places as far as California and Colorado.

Moreover, introducing the bear has little scientific merit. The Fish and Wildlife Service has not shown how the grizzly is vital to the survival of the ecosystem of the Selway-Bitteroot. In fact, no solid evidence proves that the bear once roamed there in great numbers. Some have pointed to a supposed journal entry by Lewis and Clark claiming that they shot around 20 grizzly in the area during their travels. Considering that no taxonomy was even in place at the time to distinguish between types of bears, it is ludicrous to use a journal entry almost 200 years ago as a solid basis of the facts. Finally, the small amount of data that does exist from previous attempts to capture and release grizzly into unfamiliar and rugged terrain shows that it is impossible to predict the behavioral response of the bear. I believe it is not worth the cost, both in human and budgetary terms, to find out. Mr. Speaker, considering the significant amount of opposition to, and the lack of scientific need for the proposed grizzly introduction, we must look again at what is clearly the real impetus behind this idea. Introducing the bears addresses only an emotional attachment to the romance of having grizzly bears roaming the wilderness. It contributes to Mr. Babbitt's realization of the spiritual dream that he envisioned with his Hopi Indian friend so many years ago.

If environmentalists get their way with the grizzlies, there will be a devastating impact on the freedoms and livelihoods of my constituents, and significant ramifications throughout this country. I have seen evidence lately of ambitious goals by the Fish and Wildlife Service and environmental groups to populate regions of the West with thousands of grizzly bears. This would have the drastic consequence of shutting down access to many of our lands and forests to all human activity, including hiking and camping which virtually all Americans enjoy from time to time.

This would be a giant step closer to the utopia religious environmentalists are striving to create—a utopia where human beings have only as much value as the razorback sucker fish, and possibly less.

Mr. Speaker, this religious vision is not shared by every American and no American should be forced to promote a religious vision contrary to their own beliefs. The environmentalists want a new Inquisition to eradicate those with opposing views, and they have the might of the Executive behind them. This threatens, in the most profound way, our entire way of life. It is thoroughly un-American, and I won't stand for it.

IV. RACE

DIALOGUE, INTERACTION, AND COMMITMENT[1]
James H. Paige III

Cabinet Secretary and Tax Commissioner, West Virginia Department of Tax and Revenue; born 1960, Wheeling, WV; A.B., Bethany College, 1982, and M.A., University of Pittsburgh, 1983; J.D., West Virginia University, 1987; trust administrator, Pittsburgh National Bank, 1987–89; selected among nation's 50 black leaders of the future by Ebony *magazine, 1990.*

Editors' introduction: On October 22, 1995, James H. Paige III gave the keynote address on racism before the 115th annual Governing Assembly of the West Virginia Council of Churches, Charleston, West Virginia. Council members are Methodist, Episcopal, Roman Catholic, Orthodox, Disciples of Christ, Church of the Brethren, Lutheran, Presbyterian, Salvation Army, United Church of Christ, and West Virginia Baptist Convention delegates. Bob Schwarz of the *Charleston Gazette* (Oct. 21, 1995) reported that "the Council of Churches has a long history of taking positions on issues affecting West Virginians." The theme of the conference was, "Let the Mountains Ring With the Harmony of Liberty," from James Weldon Johnson's hymn, "Lift Every Voice and Sing." Anticipating Paige's speech, Father John McDonnell of St. Agnes Catholic Church in Kanawha City, West Virginia, stated: "Look around and you'll see a society taut with racial tension. And we can say, this is a place for the church to be active and see one another as brothers and sisters." In a letter dated August 2, 1995 sent to Paige, William B. Allen, officer of the Council of Churches, explained that the day after his speech, there would be "small break-out groups that will continue the dialogue and seek to develop a Council of Churches statement on the issue of racism." Schwarz noted that the Governing Assembly had proclaimed that racism is "an evil which endures in our society

---

[1]Delivered at the John XXIII Pastoral Center, Charleston, WV, on October 22, 1995, at 7:30 p.m.

and in our churches. . . . We call upon the churches and all West Virginians to recognize racism and to exercise every means to overcome it."

Paige read from a prepared manuscript in the John XXIII Pastoral Center to approximately 150 people. He informed the editors of this volume that he "utilized history to initially develop his narrative; then used quotes, examples, and direct challenges to the audience to prompt his appeal to action." He also "received many positive comments from participants and from the Charleston community." Following his speech, Paige received questions from the floor. When U.S. Senator John D. Rockefeller IV of West Virginia printed Paige's speech in the *Congressional Record* (Jan. 26, 1996), he characterized it as "sincere, insightful, and educational. Despite America's proud history . . . we still struggle with the signs and attitudes of racism in virtually every corner of out society."

James H. Paige III's speech: It is indeed an honor to be asked to participate in your Annual Governing Assembly.

I have been intrigued with the forum which has been organized here and impressed that you set aside a special time to discuss the hopes and concerns of West Virginia's spiritual community.

I was asked to speak here tonight about racism.

It is a topic that deserves our most intellectual thoughts and energies.

Historically, as you know, in the 1860's the most divisive issue in the United States was slavery.

The issue of slavery divided the nation.

The industrial North had very little use for slave labor.

However, the agricultural South had a great need for a large slave labor pool.

At that time, slavery was based strictly on race.

The Civil War was fought and the slave issue was settled, but the issue of racism was not resolved.

Even after the Civil War and during the reconstruction period, our nation still struggled with the issue of racism.

Because even *after* slavery, we had a legacy of Jim Crow laws—of segregation—and this issue of racism was based purely on color.

So, although the Civil War was over, our nation was still confused about Lincoln's notion that "Four score and seven years ago, our fathers brought forth on this continent a new nation conceived in liberty and dedicated to the proposition that *all* men were created equal."

And over 100 years later, in the 1950's and 60's, the nation was *still* divided by race.

As a result, there was a whole movement led by the Civil Rights leader Dr. Martin Luther King, Jr. who was basically trying to get America to live up to the Constitution.

As Lincoln had noted earlier, our preamble states "We hold these truths to be self-evident—that all men our created equal."

From a historical perspective I think it interesting that during the 1860's there was a strong polarization based on slavery.

And in the 1960's that polarization still existed—not on slavery, however, but on segregation, in an attempt to separate our races.

So the Civil Rights movement resulted in legislation that was to end this segregation.

Therefore, we experienced a desegregation of schools, of public facilities.

We now have laws on the books that make segregation illegal.

We come to an interesting stage in this brief historical perspective, because what the laws could not do were to change racial attitudes—the way people think and the way people feel about each other.

Although tremendous strides have been made, even 30 years after the great Civil Rights movement, the issue of racism is still prevalent in our society today.

The recent O. J. Simpson trial and verdict brought back to the surface again this cancer of racism.

But the questions that still lingers "What is racism and how do we solve it?"

How do we define racism?

In order to deal with a problem, we should try to define it first.

I define it as an attitude people have in which they feel they are superior to another group of people . . .

And *that* superiority gives them certain privileges of authority over those people. Now the result of racism is that the people who have been victimized by racism respond with bitterness and resentment toward those who exercise that authority.

And, the alienation becomes even greater. So, if you think about it in a logical fashion, racism is based purely on ignorance.

Because racism takes one criteria, a superficial criteria—race—and it passes judgment on an entire group of people.

Utilizing folklore, tradition, and stereotypes—not facts, not any type of intellectual analysis—racism concludes that all the people in a certain classification are a certain way.

I think we all could conclude that this type of deductive reasoning is unwise and unproductive.

Whether it's black against white, whether it's white against black—it doesn't matter.

This type of attitude is unproductive, unhealthy and undeserved in our society today.

Now that we have defined the issue, how do we find solutions to address this evil?

I don't believe racism is an issue that our government can solve.

Because government cannot legislate morality.

Government cannot tell people to think a certain way or feel a certain way.

When our government attempts to legislate feelings and attitudes, it creates greater problems.

In America, our great land of freedom and independence in which we live, we hold it as a high value and virtue that people can think thoughts they want to think and feel the way they want to feel—they have certain liberties and certain freedoms.

And rightly so.

The only danger of this is that when people have racial thoughts and racial feelings, it creates a tremendous hardship for society.

So, if government cannot solve this problem, how can we address this major issue of racism in our society today?

I think this is an issue that can only be resolved with a continuing dialogue, interaction and commitment.

Racism is an activity that requires daily moral awakening that leads to real change.

The only way we can overcome the stereotypes, the tradition, the false information we have been given about each other is through contact with the people we have learned to disdain and look down upon.

There is nothing government can do about that.

There is no way we can legislate that black people and white people must sit down together, and learn about each other, understand each other, and appreciate each other's differences.

Integration certainly went a long way in bringing our races together.

But further steps are needed to change attitudes.

Because racism is not genetic—it's a learned value system, it is an attitude that is passed down from one generation to the next.

It's a cancer which continues to rob our nation of its productivity.

If we didn't have to deal with the barrier of racism, imagine the energy, talent and resources which could be directed toward solving problems in our society which are universal and common to all of us.

Now let's examine some solutions to breaking this barrier of racism.

First and foremost, I think one has to address this issue openly and honestly on an individual basis using self-anaysis. Let me state I don't think there is anything wrong with cherishing your own race—your own culture and values—but the issue is whether you respect others who do the same.

In order to have racial harmony in our culture today, we must respect our differences.

Actually, to have harmony, we *must have* differences.

For example, in the world of music.

You could have an orchestra—which has stringed instruments, percussion instruments—each instrument has its own distinct sound but because they are playing from the same score, and they are contributing what they were designed to contribute, that creates a very harmonious sound which is very pleasing to the ear.

Again, they are not competing with each other, they are complimenting each other.

In like manner, we can have racial harmony by respecting the fact that we come from different cultural orientations and different historical experiences.

But what we bring to the whole, creates something we could not have apart from each other.

What we collectively bring together could be much stronger and could be much better than what the individual groups would have independently.

Frederick Douglass once said, "We are one, our cause is one, and we must help each other; if we are to succeed."

And that's the real beauty of America—that we are stronger together as a nation than we are apart.

The next step in addressing solutions toward the issue of racism in our society is one of *education*.

And I feel that this educational component is the most important component because it starts in the home with parents teaching their children about respecting not only their own race but respecting other races as well. . . .

Teaching them to love their neighbors as they would love themselves . . .

Teaching them to respect people who are different than themselves . . .

Teaching them to recognize that every individual has some intrinsic value and worth.

For me, growing up as an African-American in a predominately white City and State, I learned at a very early age to appreciate different cultures because of my parents and my friends.

Although I was raised in a culture which was not as economically affluent as others in which I was exposed, I still maintained a high degree of respect for both cultures.

Because, *my* goal as I got older was to pull from the strength of both cultures to be the best person I could possibly be.

And it's important to note, that one of the severe consequences of racism is that it robs people from being the best they can possibly be

Because racism does not allow people to pull from the strengths of others.

Therefore, education at home and education in school is the key to opening our minds, to breaking-down stereotypes, myths and folklore about other cultures.

Because education is the key, I extend to you an opportunity to work with me.

I have established several Learning Centers around the state with the primary focus of educating our young people about the difference education can make in their lives.

I invite you to come and share your experiences with these children who come from different cultures and races.

Together we can learn from each other and attack the problems which we are finding in our communities—illiteracy, juvenile delinquency, ignorance.

I'm sure most of you would agree, that these young people are worth saving.

And as influential leaders, as spiritual leaders, I believe that "giving back" to your individual communities will do more to eradicate racism than all of the marches and trials put together.

Your example as a role model in your community is very influential when children are small, but it certainly does not stop there.

It is very critical for a young person to have someone to turn to for guidance when they reach an age that they are making the big choices that will influence their future. . . .

Whether to stay in school or drop-out, whether to stick with their gang or try to move on as an individual, whether to try to hold a job or make money some easier, more dangerous way.

Someone of this age can really benefit from association with a mentor—an adult with valuable life experience who can guide a young person through some of the tough decisions that he will have to make.

Some schools or churches have formal programs where individuals are paired based on common interests or goals.

An adult who is a physical therapist, for example, may be paired with a young person who is interested in pursuing a career in the health field.

The adult knows what it will take in practical terms for a person to achieve this goal and is, therefore, a tremendous resource for a young person to have for encouragement.

If there is such a program in your area, I urge you to consider becoming involved.

If there is not, keep your eyes open for ways that you can support the dreams of young people around you.

Dr. William Julius Wilson, the sociologist, grew up poor.

His father died when he was twelve.

He was the oldest of six children.

When asked how he was able to achieve under such circumstances, he said:

"I was able to get out of that situation because first of all, I always had a role model out there. . . .

My aunt Janice

Who was the first person in our family to get a college education . . .

She used to take me to museums and give me books to read and so on.

And then I served as a role model for my other brothers and sisters."

This speaks powerfully to the tremendous influence that a role model can have on a person's life. There are countless opportunities for you to put the skills you've learned in life to use helping others make their way.

And I am really convinced that this is where all real change, all real building for the future takes place—on a very personal level right around you.

In the past, some communities have sunk deeper and deeper into decay, waiting for someone to come to the rescue.

I say, "We are our own rescuers.

We are the ones who will save ourselves."

We can hope for money or assistance to come from somewhere.

Sometimes it does and sometimes it doesn't.

But we cannot afford to sit and wait.

We must do what we can, what is within our power, to make our communities sounder, our children's lives more promising.

We need to take advantage of every program that is currently in operation to make our streets safer and our futures brighter.

We are the ones who live in our neighborhoods.

If we do not care enough to do our very best to make that place a good area in which to live, then why should we expect others to?

We have the most to gain by working to improve our communities and the most to lose by sitting back and waiting.

If we want better lives, then the very first step is doing what each one of us can do to make positive things happen.

Start with you, with your family, your street, this church.

We must first be responsible for ourselves and our activities.

Then sometimes you find that changes that occur in small places often lead to dramatic changes in wider areas.

You never know where your example and influence will lead.

But I do know that for any of it to be successful, for any change to occur, we must commit to this cause and lead others to do the same.

When speaking out on racism, Senator Bill Bradley from New Jersey said most people are supportive and say, "I'm glad you said that."

"But this is not a spectator sport," he says, "This is an activity that requires daily moral awakening as well as a commitment that leads to real change."

As spiritual leaders, you know better than anyone what your communities need.

You know where you need literacy training.

You know where you need paint and brooms and willing hands to clean up.

You know where you need recreational programs to keep kids off the streets.

It is up to each and every one of us to begin to address these problems with the resources that we have available to us.

Certainly government needs to be involved, but we are the main sources of power.

The many needs of the country's citizens must be addressed on a national level.

But right here is where it all starts.

We live here

Work here

Play here. We, as members of the human race, are the ones who must first make improving our lives a priority.

We are the primary builders of our better lives.

It is a unique experience for me to address such an influential group of West Virginians.

And it is an experience that makes me very proud.

When I look out at all of you, I see the faces of men who want what is best for the people around them . . .

Their spouses . . .

Children . . .

Parents . . .

And neighbors.

You may say that the little bit of power you do yield is not enough to make any concrete changes.

You may say that it doesn't have the money behind it to make it effective.

You may say it is not enough to change the world.

I say that it is.

The power that you have as an individual man can change the way that your wife thinks about herself and her value as a partner who works beside you.

You have the power to create a home where your children know that they are safe and loved and will be supported in all their efforts to grow up to be caring, responsible people.

You have the power to make your neighbors feel they are not alone, that someone is watching out for them.

Within your family, *you* have the power to cease making distinctions and placing value using those differences.

Maybe you are not the mayor or a famous athlete or a wealthy contributor to charity.

But you are a person who influences the quality of every life he touches in small ways and in large ways.

Use that power constructively.

Use the tools that God gave you to change your world for the better.

And this is how I answer the question, "How do we teach our children how to deal with racism?"

A change for our futures and our children's futures must come from me and you.

Society's rules should change, and eventually I think they probably will.

But think of the time wasted while we sat waiting for that miraculous day to happen.

I feel we are all called to be citizens of action. Today is the day . . .

Now is the best times . . .

To start building that new life.

In closing, I commend your organization's effort here this evening, because we all know that Jesus's ministry is one of reconciliation.

We will soon enter into our fourth century as a nation.

Whether we build in that fourth century a civilization we can be proud of depends on whether we can arrive at a common conception of what that civilization might stand for or what it might do superbly well.

It really depends on us and our children.

The mantle of leadership has fallen on our shoulders. So let's make this event more than just a dinner and a key-note speech.

Let's allow it to be the first building-block in over-coming this barrier of racism.

Thank you.

BRIDGING THE RACIAL DIVIDE[2]
VERNON E. JORDAN, JR.

Senior partner, Akin, Gump, Strauss, Hauer, and Feld, L.L.P, Washington, D.C., 1981 to present; born, 1935, Atlanta, GA; B.A., De-Pauw University, 1957; J. D., Howard University, 1960; NAACP, 1952; President, National Urban League; Executive Director, United Negro College Fund; Georgia Field Director, NAACP; Rockefeller Foundation; honorary degrees.

Editors' introduction: The Executive Leadership Council and Foundation is an association of African-American executives at Fortune 500 companies. The Leadership Council fosters African-Americans in senior level positions throughout corporate America. In addition to serving as co-chair for the Leadership Council's seventh annual recognition dinner, on October 26, 1995, Washington, D.C., Jordan gave the keynote address that is printed below. Reading from a manuscript, he spoke to approximately 1,500 people in a banquet room of the Washington Hilton Towers. In attendance were members of the Executive Leadership Council and their guests, members of Congress, and African-American corporate leaders.

Addressing "the new leadership classes which now exist within the black community," Jordan informed the editors of this volume that his purpose was to "make the audience think about the implications of attacks on affirmative action," the O. J. Simpson verdict, and the Million Man March. In June 1995, the Supreme Court had ruled against preference programs based on race or

---

[2]Delivered at the Washington Hilton Towers, Washington, D.C., on October 26, 1995 at 8:30 p.m.

sex, and race-configured Congressional districts. A prolonged trial-by-television of O. J. Simpson, polarized many along racial lines when Simpson was acquitted. On October 16, 1995, Louis Farrakhan, Minister of the Nation of Islam in America, sponsored the Million Man March in Washington, D.C., in which he concluded that "white supremacy has poisoned the bloodstream of U.S. institutions, and there is no way that we can integrate into white supremacy and hold our dignity as human beings" (Cable News Network). Jordan wanted the audience to think about "their responsibility in the aftermath of those events." He discussed "America's racial divide, one that threatens our progress as a nation."

Jordan's speech received a "standing, rousing ovation." The speech was published in *Focus: Monthly Magazine of the Joint Center for Political and Economic Studies*, Oct./Nov. 1995, and *Vital Speeches*, Jan. 15, 1996. When he printed a segment of Jordan's speech in the *Congressional Record* (Nov.13, 1995), Representative Louis Stokes praised the address as being "insightful and very timely . . . I . . . hope that my colleagues and others throughout the Nation will . . . consider his commentary on this important issue." Stokes noted that Jordan "enjoys a close association with members of the leadership council and others who are committed to diversity in the workplace." Mr. John H. Bryan, Chair and Chief Executive Officer of the Sara Lee Corporation for twenty-one years, and fellow-southerner and friend and co-chair with Jordan, also spoke on this occasion; he advocated "affirmative action from a business standpoint." Bryan portrayed his own speech as a "warm-up act" for Jordan's address.

Vernon E. Jordan, Jr.'s speech: These are, as the old Chinese curse has it, "Interesting times." First came the attacks on affirmative action. Then, the O. J. Simpson verdict. Most recently, the Million Man March.

Suddenly, race relations—which had been invisible—have moved to center stage.

Suddenly, the idea of a color blind America in which race no longer matters much has been exposed as a fantasy.

Suddenly, settled notions about the role of race in our lives and in our society have been thrust into a sea of doubt and contradictory feelings.

This evening, I'd like to do a little thinking out loud about this confused and confusing situation with the members of the executive leadership council.

Like many others, I'm trying to make some sense of the tremendous events of the past several weeks, and I have to tell you I'm not getting far.

But I am not alone—just about everything I've heard or read about those events tells me that no one else has, either.

That may be because events are at odds with the conventional thinking about race by blacks and whites on all points of the political spectrum.

All Americans must now confront the Kerner commission's warning that we are becoming "two societies, one black, one white—separate and unequal."

And all Americans must be shaken by the strength of intolerance and extremism, and by the threat of retreat into racial isolation.

So long as black and white Americans continue to see each other as stereotypes and not as people with the same dreams, ambitions, and values, this nation will be frozen in suspicion and hate.

Unless people of good will can move swiftly to bridge the racial divide, the short term emotional charge many black Americans felt in recent weeks may turn into increased suffering over the long term.

For example, the net result of the Simpson trial could be revised criminal laws that compromise the rights of the accused and put more of our young people behind bars.

And the net result of the March could be that both whites and blacks succumb to the siren song of separatism, and get trapped in the false assumption that the problems of the black community are self-inflicted and only solvable through black spiritual renewal.

Self-renewal is critical to black progress. But so is a concerted, bi-racial attack on the social and economic causes of black disadvantage and alienation.

The truth is that we can't solve America's racial problems separately, for at the root of those problems is separation itself. The solution lies not in withdrawal but in reaching out.

But that view is in danger of becoming irrelevant in the wake of a successful march expressly limited to black men.

So we need to look at why it happened, and why it was so successful. I do not fully understand it. But I do know that the March reflects something deep and profound that is going on in America today.

An analogue to the March is the growth of the predominantly white Promise Keepers movement, which fills stadiums with masses of men affirming their faith and responsibilities.

There seems to be a yearning for spiritual renewal in America that crosses the racial divide and finds expression movements like the Million Man March, the promise keepers, and others.

Are these male-oriented movements reaction to the new role of women in our economic life and the change in family structures?

Do they derive from economic insecurity driven by vast technological changes that have shattered old certainties and economic relationships?

When people are caught in the throes of sweeping economic changes beyond their control, and when income inequality shakes their self-image, they often turn to spiritual pursuits and traditional values.

And where will such movements go from here? Will a withdrawal to spiritual concerns mean abandonment of such public concerns as economic justice and social integration?

One might understand the March's stress on atonement in that light. What is atonement? Does it presume that it is wrong to pursue the American dream of a little white house with green shutters and a white picket fence, a car in the garage, a TV in the den, beer in the cooler, tuition for the children, two weeks at the beach and a debt-free estate?

That question is relevant because most of the marchers were middle class—they were younger, better educated, and more affluent than most black people.

Did the March have a political component? The polls found that four out of five marchers were registered to vote. Will they retain their commitment to the political process and intensify it by getting others to register and vote?

Finally, I have to ask whether the March was just another one of those "feel-good" events, where people let off steam and marching substitutes for concrete action to change the root causes of their dilemma.

Words are no substitute for action. But the March was a form of action—people traveled to the capital, disrupted their daily lives, pledged to act differently and behaved with great dignity.

And yet, the March remains shrouded in ambiguity.

If I am right in thinking that it reflects something going on in America that transcends race, then we need to figure out what it is and how to use it positively for black people and the nation.

That's a job for the institutions in our community equipped with the researchers and know-how to do it—the Joint Center, Howard University, and other repositories of black intellectual prowess. They can help us understand this new, elusive spirit of our times, and help us decide upon a course of action.

But as we do, we must also understand the roles and functions of the division of labor in our community, especially as they have changed since the 1960s.

For there are now five distinct new leadership classes that have arisen alongside the traditional ones of Du Bois' "talented tenth," such as the black church, the press, the colleges, and the civil rights groups.

These new leadership groups include:

One, black elected officials, many of whose constituents are white, Hispanic and Asian.

Two, managers of predominantly white institutions, ranging from school superintendents and police chiefs to foundation heads, college presidents, and cabinet officers.

Three, indigenous community leadership, whose local organizations represent welfare families, public housing tenants, and other community-based entities, and whose backgrounds are similar to those of their constituents.

Four, black entrepreneurs who produce goods and services for markets that extend beyond the black community.

Five, blacks in corporate America, as exemplified by the Executive Leadership Council.

These new leadership groups all share the experience of negotiating the deep and sometimes treacherous waters of majority institutions. Thus, they are well situated to bring a wider perspective to the issues.

That perspective is necessary if we are to make progress without being ensnared in futile arguments about self-defeating separatism and blind nationalism.

The new leadership groups can help inoculate us against dem-
agoguery and extremism. They can bring powerful assets such as
resources, skills and knowledge of the world beyond the confines
of dysfunctional communities. Hopefully, they can help answer
the question asked in such pain and wonder in the heart of the
ghetto—"Is there no balm in Gilead? Is there no physician there?"

As we assess the March, we should recall the words written
many years ago by the great black historian, Carter G. Woodson:

"The race needs workers, not leaders," Woodson wrote. "If
we can finally succeed in translating the idea of leadership into
that of service, we may find it possible to lift the Negro to a higher
level."

Perhaps that is the true meaning of the March—the yearning
of so many black men to be of service to the community.

But what about those who were not invited to the March—
black women, white people, Hispanics, Asians—all of whom must
participate in America's renewal and in bridging the gap between
the races.

They must not be ignored, for the gap cannot be closed without them . . . because the only sane course of action lies within
the context of an open, pluralistic, integrated society.

In "The Invisible Man," Ralph Ellison wrote: "Our fate is to
become one, and yet many. This is not prophecy, but
description."

We are a long way from that goal, and the path to it is an ardu-
ous one. There will be diversions along the route from both white
racists and black separatists.

But it is the only route that leads to the attainable goal and
to a goal worth attaining.

From time to time, it will be tempting to withdraw from the
struggle, to seek solace in the warmth and comfort of one's own
community. But in the long run we cannot do the segregationists'
work for them by excluding ourselves from our fair portion of the
society we helped build. Nor can we allow white institutions such
as corporate America to abandon the struggle. We must work toward "the beloved community," black and white together.

Those are some of the thoughts that come to mind as I've
pondered the strange, changing state of race relations today.

I hope you—the Executive Leadership Council—will partake
in the action and the passion of our turbulent times, dedicated to
service and to building an open, pluralistic, integrated Society.

TEARING AT THE HEART OF AMERICA[3]
WILLIAM J. CLINTON

President of the United States; born 1947, Hope, AR; B.S., 1968, Georgetown University; Rhodes Scholar, Oxford University, 1968–70; J.D., Yale University, 1973; Governor of Arkansas, 1979–81, 1983–92.

Editors' introduction: On October 16, 1995, President Clinton addressed the issue of race in the Liz Sutherland Carpenter Lecture sponsored by the Erwin Center, College of Liberal Arts, and the Texas Union Distinguished Speakers Committee of the University of Texas. Clinton spoke at the Erwin Center to 12,000 people including students, faculty, members of the State Legislature and Congress, and leaders from various organizations and companies from across Texas. The speech was televised by C-Span. Ms. Carpenter, former Press Secretary and Staff Director to Lady Bird Johnson, informed the editors of this volume that the President's speech received a "fabulous response."

Earlier, on July 19, 1995, at the Rotunda of the National Archives in Washington, D.C., Clinton had startled many with his decisive defense of affirmative action. Perceived by some to have equivocated on some issues, in this Archives address, Clinton argued that "affirmative action has been good for America," and pledged to restore "the American dream of opportunity." Rev. Jesse Jackson praised Clinton's stand; the response of the black community generally varied (Derrick Z. Jackson, *Boston Globe*, July 21, 1995).

The same day that Clinton gave the Texas speech, Louis Farrakhan, Minister of the Nation of Islam in America, held his Million Man March in Washington, D.C. Farrakhan alluded to Clinton's speech earlier that day: "Now the president . . . wanted to heal the great divide. But I respectfully suggest to the president, you did not dig deep enough at the malady that divides black and white in order to affect a solution to the problem."

[3]Delivered at the Erwin Center, the University of Texas, Austin, TX, on October 16, 1995, at 9:34 a.m.

When a reporter asked Mike McCurry, Press Secretary, why the President did not mention Louis Farrakhan and Mark Furman [a police detective who testified at the O.J. Simpson trial] McCurry answered, "Clinton had transcended those personalities who are divisive so that we could find ways which Americans can come together on these issues." Journalists asked how the President prepared to discuss the Million Man March on such short notice. McCurry explained that, when writing the Texas address, Clinton consulted with Jesse Jackson, who also spoke at the Million Man March, John Lewis, Ron Brown, Vernon Jordan, Jr., Duval Patrick, Ernie Green, and Alexis Herman. Speech writers David Shipley and Terry Edmunds, under Don Baer, worked primarily upon the Texas lecture, with the President writing large portions. "He was making blue felt-tip changes and rewriting passages until the early hours this morning, and then woke up about 7:00 a.m. . . . and worked on it some more. . . . It is a speech very much from the heart" (transcript of press briefing). In this Texas address, Clinton examined the "persistence of racism, hatred, and division, and called for unity and reconciliation."

President Clinton's speech: Thank you. You know, when I was a boy growing up in Arkansas, I thought it highly—(applause)—I thought it highly unlikely that I would ever become President of the United States. Perhaps the only thing even more unlikely was that I should ever have the opportunity to be cheered at the University of Texas. (Applause.) I must say I am very grateful for both of them.(Laughter.)

President Berdahl, Chancellor Cunningham, Dean Olson; to the Texas Longhorn Band, thank you for playing Hail to the Chief. (Applause.) You were magnificent. (Applause.) To my longtime friend of nearly 25 years now, Bernard Rappaport, thank you for your statement and your inspiration and your life of generous giving to this great university and so many other good causes. (Applause.)

All the distinguished guests in the audience—I hesitate to start—but I thank my friend and your fellow Texan, Henry Cisneros, for coming down here with me and for his magnificent work as Secretary of HUD. (Applause.)

I thank you Congressman, Lloyd Doggett, and his wife, Libby, for flying down with me. (Applause.) And I'm glad to see my dear friend, Congressman Jake Pickle here. I miss you. (Applause.) Your Attorney General, Dan Morales; the Land Commissioner, Garry Mauro—I thank all of them for being here. (Applause.)

Thank you, Lucy Johnson, for being here. (Applause.) And please give my regards to your wonderful mother. (Applause.)

I have not seen her—there she is. And I have to recognize and thank your former Congresswoman and now distinguished Professor Barbara Jordan for the magnificent job you did on the immigration issue. (Applause.) Thank you so much. (Applause.) Thank you. Thank you. (Applause.)

My wife told me about coming here so much, I wanted to come and see for myself. I also know, as all of you do, that there is no such thing as saying no to Liz Carpenter. (Laughter.) I drug it out as long as I could just to hear a few more jokes. (Laughter.)

My fellow Americans, I want to begin by telling you that I am hopeful about America. When I looked at Nikole Bell up here introducing me, and I shook hands with these other young students—I looked into their eyes; I saw the AmeriCorps button on that gentlemen's shirt—(applause)—I was reminded, as I talk about this thorny subject of race today, I was reminded of what Winston Churchill said about the United States when President Roosevelt was trying to pass the Lend-Lease Act so that we could help Britain in their war against Nazi Germany before we, ourselves, were involved. And for a good while the issue was hanging fire. And it was unclear whether the Congress would permit us to help Britain, who at that time was the only bulwark against tyranny in Europe.

And Winston Churchill said, "I have great confidence in the judgment and the common sense of the American people and their leaders. They invariably do the right thing after they have examined every other alternative." (Laughter.) So I say to you, let me begin by saying that I can see in the eyes of these students and in the spirit of this moment, we will do the right thing.

In recent weeks, every one of us has been made aware of a simple truth—white Americans and black Americans often see the same world in drastically different ways—ways that go beyond and beneath the Simpson trial and its aftermath, which brought these perceptions so starkly into the open.

The rift we see before us that is tearing at the heart of America exists in spite of the remarkable progress black Americans have made in the last generation, since Martin Luther King swept

America up in his dream, and President Johnson spoke so powerfully for the dignity of man and the destiny of democracy in demanding that Congress guarantee full voting rights to blacks.
The rift between blacks and whites exists still in a very special way
in America, in spite of the fact that we have become much more
racially and ethnically diverse, and that Hispanic Americans—
themselves no strangers to discrimination—are now almost 10
percent of our national population.

The reasons for this divide are many. Some are rooted in the
awful history and stubborn persistence of racism. Some are rooted in the different ways we experience the threats of modern life
to personal security, family values, and strong communities.
Some are rooted in the fact that we still haven't learned to talk
frankly, to listen carefully, and to work together across racial
lines.

Almost 30 years ago, Dr. Martin Luther King took his last
march with sanitation workers in Memphis. They marched for
dignity, equality, and economic justice. Many carried placards
that read simply, "I am a man." The throngs of men marching in
Washington today, almost all of them, are doing so for the same
stated reason. But there is a profound difference between this
march today and those of 30 years ago. Thirty years ago, the
marchers were demanding the dignity and opportunity they were
due because in the face of terrible discrimination, they had
worked hard, raised their children, paid their taxes, obeyed the
laws, and fought our wars.

Well, today's march is also about pride and dignity and respect. But after a generation of deepening social problems that
disproportionately impact black Americans, it is also about black
men taking renewed responsibility for themselves, their families,
and their communities. (Applause.) It's about saying no to crime
and drugs and violence. It's about standing up for atonement and
reconciliation. It's about insisting that others do the same, and offering to help them. It's about the frank admission that unless
black men shoulder their load, no one else can help them or their
brothers, their sisters, and their children escape the hard, bleak
lives that too many of them still face.

Of course, some of those in the march do have a history that
is far from its message of atonement and reconciliation. One million men are right to be standing up for personal responsibility.
But one million men do not make right one man's message of mal-

ice and division. (Applause.) No good house was ever built on a bad foundation. Nothing good ever came of hate. So let us pray today that all who march and all who speak will stand for atonement, for reconciliation, for responsibility.

Let us pray that those who have spoken for hatred and division in the past will turn away from that past and give voice to the true message of those ordinary Americans who march. If that happens—(applause)—if that happens, the men and the women who are there with them will be marching into better lives for themselves and their families. And they could be marching into a better future for America. (Applause.)

Today we face a choice—one way leads to further separation and bitterness and more lost futures. The other way, the path of courage and wisdom, leads to unity, to reconciliation, to a rich opportunity for all Americans to make the most of the lives God gave them. This moment in which the racial divide is so clearly out in the open need not be a setback for us. It presents us with a great opportunity, and we dare not let it pass us by. (Applause.)

In the past when we've had the courage to face the truth about our failure to live up to our own best ideals, we've grown stronger, moved forward and restored proud American optimism. At such turning points America moved to preserve the union and abolished slavery; to embrace women's suffrage; to guarantee basic legal rights to America without regard to race, under the leadership of President Johnson. At each of these moments, we looked in the national mirror and we're brave enough to say, this is not who we are; we're better than that.

Abraham Lincoln reminded us that a house divided against itself cannot stand. When divisions have threatened to bring our house down, somehow we have always moved together to shore it up. My fellow Americans, our house is the greatest democracy in all human history. And with all its racial and ethical diversity, it has beaten the odds of human history. But we know that divisions remain, and we still have work to do. (Applause.)

The two worlds we see now each contain both truth and distortion. Both black and white Americans must face this, for honesty is the only gateway to the many acts of reconciliation that will unite our worlds at last into one America.

White America must understand and acknowledge the roots of black pain. It began with unequal treatment first in law and later in fact. African Americans indeed have lived too long with a justice system that in too many cases has been and continues to be less than just. (Applause.) The record of abuses extends from lynchings and trumped up charges to false arrests and police brutality. The tragedies of Emmett Till and Rodney King are bloody markers on the very same road.

Still today too many of our police officers play by the rules of the bad old days. It is beyond wrong when law—abiding black parents have to tell their law-abiding children to fear the police whose salaries are paid by their own taxes. (Applause.)

And blacks are right to think something is terribly wrong when African American men are many times more likely to be victims of homicide than any other group in this country; when there are more African American men in our corrections system than in our colleges; when almost one in three African American men in their 20s are either in jail, on parole or otherwise under the supervision of the criminal justice system—nearly one in three. And that is a disproportionate percentage in comparison to the percentage of blacks who use drugs in our society. Now, I would like every white person here and in America to take a moment to think how he or she would feel if one in three white men were in similar circumstances.

And there is still unacceptable economic disparity between blacks and whites. It is so fashionable to talk today about African Americans as if they have been some sort of protected class. Many whites think blacks are getting more than their fair share in terms of jobs and promotions. That is not true. That is not true. (Applause.)

The truth is that African Americans still make on average about 60 percent of what white people do; that more than half of African American children live in poverty. And at the very time our young Americans need access to college more than ever before, black college enrollment is dropping in America.

On the other hand, blacks must understand and acknowledge the roots of white fear in America. There is a legitimate fear of the violence that is too prevalent in our urban areas; and often by experience or at least what people see on the news at night, violence for those white people too often has a black face.

It isn't racist for a parent to pull his or her child close when walking through a high-crime neighborhood, or to wish to stay away from neighborhoods where innocent children can be shot in school or standing at bus stops by thugs driving by with assault weapons or toting handguns like old west desperados. (Applause.)

It isn't racist for parents to recoil in disgust when they read about a national survey of gang members saying that two-thirds of them feel justified in shooting someone simply for showing them disrespect. It isn't racist for whites to say they don't understand why people put up with gangs on the corner or in the projects, or with drugs being sold in the schools or in the open. It's not racist for whites to assert that the culture of welfare dependency, out-of-wedlock pregnancy and absent fatherhood cannot be broken by social programs unless there is first more personal responsibility. (Applause.)

The great potential for this march today, beyond the black community, is that whites will come to see a larger truth—that blacks share their fears and embrace their convictions; openly assert that without changes in the black community and within individuals, real change for our society will not come.

This march could remind white people that most black people share their old-fashioned American values—(applause)—for most black Americans still do work hard, care for their families, pay their taxes, and obey the law, often under circumstances which are far more diffcult than those their white counterparts face. (Applause.)

Imagine how you would feel if you were a young parent in your 20s with a young child living in a housing project, working somewhere for $5 an hour with no health insurance, passing every day people on the street selling drugs, making 100 times what you make. Those people are the real heroes of America today, and we should recognize that. (Applause.)

And white people too often forget that they are not immune to the problems black Americans face—crime, drugs, domestic abuse, and teen pregnancy. They are too prevalent among whites as well, and some of those problems are growing faster in our white population than in our minority population. (Applause.)

So we all have a stake in solving these common problems together. It is therefore wrong for white Americans to do what they have done too often simply to move further away from the problems and support policies that will only make them worse. (Applause.)

Finally, both sides seem to fear deep down inside that they will never quite be able to see each other as more than enemy faces, all of whom carry at least a sliver of bigotry in their hearts. Differences of opinion rooted in different experiences are healthy, indeed essential, for democracies. But differences so great and so rooted in race threaten to divide the house Mr. Lincoln gave his life to save. As Dr. King said, "We must learn to live together as brothers, or we will perish as fools." (Applause.)

Recognizing one another's real grievances is only the first step. We must all take responsibility for ourselves, our conduct and our attitudes. America, we must clean our house of racism. (Applause.)

To our white citizens, I say, I know most of you every day do your very best by your own lights—to live a life free of discrimination. Nevertheless, too many destructive ideas are gaining currency in our midst. The taped voice of one policeman should fill you with outrage. (Applause.) And I say, we must clean the house of white America of racism. Americans who are in the white majority should be proud to stand up and be heard denouncing the sort of racist rhetoric we heard on that tape—so loudly and clearly denouncing it, that our black fellow citizens can hear us. White racism may be black people's burden, but it's white people's problem. (Applause.) We must clean our house. (Applause.)

To our black citizens, I honor the presence of hundreds of thousands of men in Washington today, committed to atonement and to personal responsibility, and the commitment of millions of other men and women who are African Americans to this cause. I call upon you to build on this effort, to share equally in the promise of America. But to do that, your house, too, must be cleaned of racism. There are too many today—(applause)—there are too many today, white and black, on the left and the right, on the steet corners and radio waves, who seek to sow division for their own purposes. To them I say, no more. We must be one. (Applause.)

Long before we were so diverse, our nation's motto was E Pluribus Unum—out of many, we are one. We must be one—as neighbors, as fellow citizens; not separate camps, but family—white, black, Latino, all of as, no matter how different, who share basic American values and are willing to live by them.

When a child is gunned down on a street in the Bronx, no matter what our race, he is our American child. When a woman dies from a beating, no matter what our race or hers, she is our American sister. (Applause.) And every time drugs course through the vein of another child, it clouds the future of all our American children. (Applause.)

Whether we like it or not, we are one nation, one family, indivisible. And for us, divorce or separation are not options. (Applause.)

Here, in 1995, on the edge of the 21st century, we dare not tolerate the existence of two Americas. Under my watch, I will do everything I can to see that as soon as possible there is only one—one America under the rule of law; one social contract committed not to winner take all, but to giving all Americans a chance to win together—one America. (Applause.)

Well, how do we get there? First, today I ask every governor, every mayor, every business leader, every church leader, every civic leader, every union steward, every student leader, most important—every citizen, in every workplace and learning place and meeting place all across America to take personal responsibility for reaching out to people of different races; for taking time to sit down and talk through this issue; to have the courage to speak honestly and frankly; and then to have the discipline to listen quietly with an open mind and an open heart, as others do the same. (Applause.)

This may seem like a simple request, but for tens of millions of Americans, this has never been a reality. They have never spoken, and they have never listened—not really, not really. (Applause.) I am convinced, based on a rich lifetime of friendships and common endeavors with people of different races, that the American people will find out they have a lot more in common than they think they do. (Applause.)

The second thing we have to do is to defend and enhance real opportunity. I'm not talking about opportunity for black Americans or opportunity for white Americans; I'm talking about opportunity for all Americans. (Applause.) Sooner or later, all our speaking, all our listening, all our caring has to lead to constructive action together for our words and our intentions to have meaning. We can do this first by truly rewarding work and family in government policies, in employment policies, in community practices.

We also have to realize that there are some areas of our country—whether in urban areas or poor rural areas like south Texas or eastern Arkansas—where these problems are going to be more prevalent just because there is no opportunity. There is only so much temptation some people can stand when they turn up against a brick wall day after day after day. And if we can spread the benefits of education and free enterprise to those who have been denied them too long and who are isolated in enclaves in this country, then we have a moral obligation to do it. It will be good for our county. (Applause.)

Third and perhaps most important of all, we have to give every child in this country, and every adult who still needs it, the opportunity to get a good education. (Applause.) President Johnson understood that; and now that I am privileged to have this job and to look back across the whole sweep of American history, I can appreciate how truly historic his commitment to the simple idea that every child in this country ought to have an opportunity to get a good, safe, decent, fulfilling education was. It was revolutionary then, and it is revolutionary today. (Applause.)

Today that matters more than ever. I'm trying to do my part. I am fighting hard against efforts to roll back family security, aid to distressed communities, and support for education. I want it to be easier for poor children to get off to a good start in school, not harder. I want it to be easier for everybody to go to college and stay there, not harder. (Applause.) I want to mend affirmative action, but I do not think America is at a place today where we can end it. The evidence of the last several weeks shows that. (Applause.)

But let us remember, the people marching in Washington today are right about one fundamental thing—at its base, this issue of race is not about government or political leaders; it is about what is in the heart and the minds and life of the American people. There will be no progress in the absence of real responsibility on the part of all Americans. Nowhere is that responsibility more important than in our efforts to promote public safety and preserve the rule of law.

Law and order is the first responsibility of government. Our citizens must respect the law and those who enforce it. Police have a life and death responsibility never, never to abuse the power granted them by the people. We know, by the way, what works in fighting crime also happens to improve relationships between the races. What works in fighting crime is community policing. We have seen it working all across America. The crime rate is down. The murder rate is down where people relate to each other across the lines of police and community in an open, honest, respectful, supportive way. We can lower crime and raise the state of race relations in America if we will remember this simple truth. (Applause.)

But if this is going to work, police departments have to be fair and engaged with, not estranged from, their communities. I am committed to making this kind of community policing a reality all across our country. But you must be committed to making it a reality in your communities. We have to root out the remnants of racism in our police departments. We've got to get it out of our entire criminal justice system. But just as the police have a sacred duty to protect the community fairly, all of our citizens have a sacred responsibility to respect the police; to teach our young people to respect them; and then to support them and work with them so that they can succeed in making us safe. (Applause.)

Let's not forget, most police officers of whatever race are honest people who love the law and put their lives on the lines so that the citizens they're protecting can lead decent, secure lives, and so that their children can grow up to do the same.

Finally, I want to say, on the day of this March, a moment about a crucial area of responsibility—the responsibility of fatherhood. The single biggest social problem in our society may be the growing absence of fathers from their children's homes, because it contributes to so many other social problems. One child in four grows up in a fatherless home. Without a father to help guide, without a father to care, without a father to teach boys to be men and to teach girls to expect respect from men, it's harder. (Applause.) There are a lot of mothers out there doing a magnificent job alone—(applause)—a magnificent job alone, but it is harder. It is harder. (Applause.) This, of course, is not a black problem or a Latino problem or a white problem; it is an American problem. But it aggravates the conditions of the racial divide.

I know from my own life it is harder because my own father died before I was born, and my stepfather's battle with alcohol kept him from being the father he might have been. But for all fathers, parenting is not easy and every parent makes mistakes. I know that, too, from my own experience. The point is that we need people to be there for their children day after day. Building a family is the hardest job a man can do, but it's also the most important.

For those who are neglecting their children, I say it is not too late; your children still need you. To those who only send money in the form of child support, I say keep sending the checks; your kids count on them, and we'll catch you and enforce the law if you stop. (Applause.) But the message of this March today—one message is that your money is no replacement for your guiding, your caring, you loving the children you brought into this world. (Applause.)

We can only build strong families when men and women respect each other; when they have partnerships; when men are as involved in the homeplace as women have become involved in the workplace. (Applause.) It means, among other things, that we must keep working until we end domestic violence against women and children. (Applause.) I hope those men in Washington today pledge among other things to never, never raise their hand in violence against a woman. (Applause.)

So today, my fellow Americans, I honor the black men marching in Washington to demonstrate their commitment to themselves, their families, and their communities. I honor the millions of men and women in America, the vast majority of every color, who without fanfare or recognition do what it takes to be good fathers and good mothers, good workers and good citizens. They all deserve the thanks of America. (Applause.)

But when we leave here today, what are you going to do? What are you going to do? Let all of us who want to stand up against racism do our part to roll back the divide. Begin by seeking out people in the workplace, the classroom, the community, the neighborhood across town, the places of worship to actually sit down and have those honest conversations I talked about—conversations where we speak openly and listen and understand how others view this world of ours.

Make no mistake about it, we can bridge this great divide. This is, after all, a very great country. And we have become great by what we have overcome. We have the world's strongest economy, and it's on the move. But we've really lasted because we have understood that our success could never be measured solely by the size of our Gross National Product. (Applause.)

I believe the march in Washington today spawned such an outpouring because it is a reflection of something deeper and stronger that is running throughout our American community. I believe that in millions and millions of different ways, our entire county is reasserting our commitment to the bedrock values that made our country great and that make life worth living.

The great divides of the past call for and were addressed by legal and legislative changes. They were addressed by leaders like

Lyndon Johnson, who passed the Civil Rights Act and the Voting Rights Act. (Applause.) And to be sure, this great divide requires a public response by democratically-elected leaders. But today we are really dealing, and we know it, with problems that grow in large measure out of the way all of us look at the world with our minds and the way we feel about the world with our hearts.

And therefore, while leaders and legislation may be important, this is work that has to be done by every single one of you. (Applause.) And this is the ultimate test of our democracy, for today the house divided exists largely in the minds and hearts of the American people. And it must be united there in the minds and hearts of our people.

Yes, there are some who would poison our progress by selling short the great character of our people and our enormous capacity to change and grow. But they will not win the day; we will win the day. (Applause.)

With your help—with your help—that day will come a lot sooner. I will do my part, but you, my fellow citizens, must do yours.

Thank you, and God bless you. (Applause.)

V. WOMEN'S RIGHTS AND ACHIEVEMENTS

COUNTRY DAY VALUES[1]
REBECCA E. MARIER

Harvard Medical School student; born New Haven, CT, 1973; diploma, Metairie Park Country Day School, Metairie, LA, l991; B.S., United States Military Academy, West Point, NY, 1995; Second Lieutenant, U.S. Army.

Editors' introduction: Second Lieutenant Rebecca Elizabeth Marier was the first woman to be graduated first in her class at the West Point Military Academy; she was first militarily, physically, and academically among those 988 persons who were graduated in 1995. She excelled over 1,000 cadets, including 130 women. Women had attended West Point since 1976, with more than 1,400 women having been commissioned second lieutenants. Upon completion of medical school at Harvard, Marier will become an Army doctor. She attended junior high and high school at the Metairie Park Country Day School in Metairie, Louisiana, where she returned on August 23, 1995, and delivered the speech printed below. When a student asked Marier about Ms. Shannon Faulkner's entrance to The Citadel, where she later withdrew because of physical problems, Marier stated that she and her lawyer "won an important legal battle for women. They have opened doors that have been closed for too long. But personally I don't think Shannon Faulkner was prepared for the physical challenges" (Eva Jacob Barkoff, *New Orleans Times-Picayune*, Sept. 7, 1995).

Marier explained to Chris Smith of *Country Day Comments* (Fall 1995) how the very good study habits she acquired at Metairie Park Country Day School had prepared her well for the challenges at West Point. "I have always been a self starter, and had a family that encouraged me during that time as a young person when you're still deciding who you are and how hard you want

<hr>

[1]Delivered at Metairie Park Country Day School, Metairie, LA, on August 23, 1995, at noon.

to work," Marier said. She advised students to "quit whining, and go out there and perform." "A goal of mine as I went through West Point," she told Smith, "was to somehow make a difference in the world. I just didn't know I'd be able to make such a difference so soon!"

Marier talked to 300 people including students convened in the school's auditorium for Junior High and High School assembly. Marier informed the editors of this volume that she "spoke with the manuscript in front of me but used it mostly for cues." Her purpose was to "share my experiences and thoughts on what helped me in my recent success at West Point. I explained my experiences and what beliefs, attitudes, and ideals helped me through them. The responses from students and teachers were extremely positive and thankful. I was a role model that students close to my age could relate to."

Rebecca E. Marier's speech: My name is Rebecca Elizabeth Marier and I am a Second Lieutenant in the US Army. I graduated from the United States Military Academy at West Point three months ago. Believe it or not—because sometimes I still can't—I graduated first in my class. I was the first woman ever to do so. Now I am entering Harvard Medical School where, if all goes well, I will graduate in four years and go on to become an Army doctor.

I spent 13 years at Country Day in the same shoes that you all are wearing right now. In August of 1978 I stepped off of a school bus . . . in the Front Circle and was shown to Room 2 by Ms. Watson. When I walk around this campus now, I am flooded with memories of what was my home away from home for so long. I think about good times on the lower school playground, English class with Mrs. Sneed, meeting Mr. Kelly when he first interviewed for the Middle School Principal job, red beans & rice on Wednesdays and donuts on Thursdays, pinball in the Grimm Gym, the senior—I mean upper school—lounge, I could go on and on. But I did not come here today to reminisce about my good old times as a Country Day Cajun.

I have often been asked why I made the choice to go to West Point. I had a number of related reasons most of which can be summed up in the Academy's motto: "Duty, Honor, Country." Duty to me means selfless service and doing what one should and morally must do. I felt then and still feel now that because I am so blessed while others in the world have so little, I have a duty to give something back to society. Honor is an ideal that I feel should be at the very core of every human being. And Country is something that so many of us take for granted. I only have to watch CNN for five minutes before I start thanking God that I was born in the USA. I wanted to be a part of a tradition of patriotism and service to this country. Of course there was one other reason why I wanted to go to the Academy, and that was the desire for a challenge. I knew that West Point would challenge me academically, physically, and mentally.

Exactly one month after I graduated from Country Day, I reported to West Point for Reception Day, the first day of Cadet Basic Training, more affectionately known to us as "Beast." I definitely got the challenge I was looking for. I remember waking on my first full day to the sound of my door being kicked open and Guns & Roses blaring, "Welcome to the Jungle" down the hallway.

The Academy spent the next six weeks of Beast welcoming me. I learned how to march, salute, and follow orders. I also qualified on an M-16 rifle and threw a hand grenade for the first time. The most important lesson that I learned that summer was the importance of helping the person next to me. Teamwork was the key to survival.

. . . That year I began the four year process of learning how to be a leader. I learned both by experience and by observation. As a group, we plebes had a number of duties, and someone in the group had to assume a leadership role and organized process. I also observed a lot of upperclassmen in their leadership positions and decided who I did and did not want to be like.

. . . I spent the following summer doing military training, learning a great deal about the various branches of the Army. For the first time, I learned how important physical fitness is to earning respect in the military. I held my own, and I watched those who didn't struggle miserably.

As sophomores, we were called yearlings. We were no longer at the bottom of the totem pole. Each of us was a team leader, which meant that we were each responsible for the progress of one plebe. More was expected of us because we were no longer new. And the academics got harder. We had a number of classmates fail classes, causing them to be separated from the Academy.

We all had so many things going on. I was taking six classes, playing on the varsity tennis team, developing a plebe, and working out to stay in good shape. I was forced to become organized and good at managing my time. No matter how organized we were, though, we all felt stressed, and we had to learn how to perform under that stress.

As time went on, I finally became a junior and eventually a senior, or Firstie. I was doing well, so as I went along, I was rewarded with more responsibility. As a Firstie, I was a regimental commander, which meant I was responsible for about 1,000 cadets.

Firstie year I got busier than I had ever imagined I could be. I had a lot going on at West Point and in addition, I was doing what all of you seniors will be doing pretty soon—applying to schools. I set my heart on going to Harvard, this time I knew if I got in, I would go. (I hoped they had forgotten me from four years before!) I waited and waited and finally, in March I got a skinny little letter with Harvard's return address on it. Somehow, I had gotten in, and I was ecstatic!

Before I knew it though, it was June 3, Graduation Day. Three days before that big day, I found out that I would be graduating first, which meant that I had the highest overall ranking academically, physically, and militarily. I got a lot of attention for being the first woman to do this—attention that I certainly didn't expect and don't know if I deserved. After all, every year someone graduates first and nobody makes a big deal about it!

. . . Ever since I can remember, I have maintained what I call my "open door/no regrets" philosophy. I haven't always known way in advance where I wanted to go or what I wanted to do with my life. But one thing is for sure. Once I find something I want, I want the door to that something to be open. I work hard to insure that I will have as many opportunities and choices as possible. I may not always succeed, and not every door will open for me, but I am determined to never have any regrets.

Because I worked hard in high school, I was accepted to West Point. But it wasn't just that. I probably could have gotten by with less studying and less diligence throughout junior high and high school. But my work paid off in a second way. Not only was I accepted to West Point, but I was extremely well prepared. I had a lot of success at the Academy because I started out with good study habits and a good base of organization skills.

Another idea that has helped me along my journey is the importance of having a "cause."

. . . My cause is a tremendous sense of obligation. For whatever reason, I was given more than my fair share of gifts. I have a strong family that taught me good values. I have had great education. I have good health. I could stand here for hours and list all that I have to be thankful for. And I know that these gifts are not free. I must find a way to make a difference and help those who have not been as fortunate as I have been. I know that if I rise to every challenge and make the most of every opportunity, I will maximize my potential and be able to give all that I owe. My cause keeps me chugging when I am tired, doubtful or discouraged. I encourage each of you to find a cause.

Finally, I want to mention an important part of my experience that I haven't discussed yet. I was a minority; West Point is only 10 percent women. We were fully integrated into the Corps of Cadets. I was not harassed, and I was treated as an equal. I learned a great lesson by being a woman in what has traditionally been a man's world. There are a lot of people out there who complain of barriers that exist as a result of racist or sexist prejudices. Some of this is legitimate. But folks, this is 1995, and people will judge you by your actions and your performance. If you feel that people do not respect you, go out and prove that you deserve their respect. Excuses and whining don't get anybody anywhere; achievements do.

OBSERVATIONS AND OPPORTUNITIES IN THE 90's[2]
CATHLEEN BLACK

President, Hearst Magazines; born Chicago, IL, 1944; B.A., Trinity College, 1966; President and CEO, Newspaper Association of America, 1991–95; President and Publisher of USA Today's parent company; honorary degrees; among "Fifty Most Powerful Women in America," Ladies' Home Journal; Ms.' Woman of the Year; Los Angeles Advertising Women's Outstanding Communicator Award.

[2]Delivered at Saint Mary's College, South Bend, IN, on June 20, 1995 at 12:45 p. m.

Editors' introduction: In her commencement speech at Wellesley College, June 1, 1990, former First Lady Barbara Bush, noted: "We are in a transitional period right now . . . learning to adjust to changes and the choices we men and women are facing." Cathleen Black, at Saint Mary's College's 148th commencement in South Bend, Indiana on June 20, 1995, then President and CEO of the Newspaper Association of America, advised graduates in her address not to be "blinded by the presumptions of others." Rather they should create their own unique potential. Black spoke in Le Mans Courtyard on the campus to 2,700 graduates along with administration, faculty, families and friends. The speech addressed issues that were timely and grounded in beliefs that reflect Saint Mary's College's misson. Black's speech was noted in *Time* magazine (June 12, 1995) and excerpted in the *New York Times* (June 4, 1995).

Cathleen Black's speech: Thank you Dr. Feigk and President Hickey . . . and good afternoon. I'm proud to be with you today . . . to share this occasion, to wear St. Mary's robe and colors.

As we meet across this podium . . . at this annual rite of graduation . . . this communal celebration of well earned accomplishment . . . Even from up here . . . I can see the warm glow of your achievement . . . mixed with a little fear . . . anticipation about the future. That, "Oh my God, what am I going to do with the rest of my life?" feeling. I see the pride of family, friends and loved ones. (And yes, maybe some bit of relief too!!)

I see a group of women who are entering the world not just with an education, but a value-centered education . . . one that has stressed the importance of learning—yes—but also of ethics, morality and service to others.

Today, I relish the opportunity to pass on a few bits of wisdom about what awaits you in the world beyond St. Mary' s warm embrace. In fact . . . I would love to tell you what you'll encounter . . . share some certainties, truths and assorted how-to's that will smooth the journey ahead. But, sorry! . . . I don't have a clue. A top advertising executive named Laurel Cutler hit the nail on the head when she said . . . "There is no data on the future."

By way of really useful advice . . . I might tell you to look both ways before you cross the street . . . to not run red lights . . . to not pet strange dogs, to not get distracted talking on a car phone while driving 60 MPH. Or I could tell you to keep your nose to the grindstone, your shoulder to the wheel . . . your ear to the ground . . . as you read the handwriting on the wall.

Or, I could give you a good lasagna recipe. Something my husband gave to a Georgetown class he was teaching . . . figuring it had more practical value than most of the foreign policy strategy he was trying to impart. Or maybe as J. Paul Getty once said when asked his secret to success . . . "Work hard . . . strike oil." So much for the really practical advice. Who knows? It might still come in handy!

But, the real reason that it's impossible to share wisdom about your future is that I don't have a crystal ball. You will encounter opportunities and obstacles that simply weren't there when I took the step in the mid-sixties that you are about to now.

And, that's the exciting part. You face a clean canvas . . . it's your own canvas . . . and whether your path takes you to work or family or both . . . it's up to you to fill it with new shapes and inspiring colors.

What I do hope I can do today is to sketch out some of the outlines. And for a group of eager, bright, accomplished women like yourselves streaming from the gates of one of America's leading colleges . . . those outlines have to be broad indeed.

There is good news and bad news. The good news is that . . . there are fewer limits and boundaries for women in shaping your lives than ever been before.

The bad news is that there are fewer limits and boundaries for women in shaping your lives than there have ever been before . . . the yin and yang of generational challenge. What the 1990s have given . . . they've also taken away. They've given you fewer preconceptions. They've taken away guarantees. They've given you wider choices. They've taken away places to hide. The end product of this yin and yang is that you are facing a new era.

In the world of work . . . we've traveled far since the 1990 *Fortune* magazine article—that's just 5 years ago that facetiously advised women that to get ahead in business they must "Look like a lady . . . act like a man . . . and work like a dog."

The work like a dog part might still hold . . . but the first two are remnants of the days when there was men's work and women's work . . . and those who crossed the line did so at their own psychic peril . . .

I remember . . . clutching my newly-minted Bachelor of Arts degree . . . setting out with cheeks flushed and heart pounding for the wilds of New York City . . . determined to launch a career in advertising and publishing. I knew I would have to knock on doors . . . but, hey . . . I thought . . . I'm smart . . . I've got the grades. After all . . . how long can it take?

What I didn't know was how many of those doors would be closed to women. In some cases, nailed shut. With the furniture piled up on the other side. And a big mean dog at the window.

Finally . . . a large ad agency offered me a break. It was as a clerk typist . . . at $65 a week. Thanks guys . . . but no thanks. Nothing wrong with that . . . but I want something more.

In time . . . I found it . . . in advertising sales for a travel magazine . . . then as the first advertising manager for a new and then ground-breaking magazine called *Ms.* . . . and after a few more jobs . . . a long and exciting tenure as publisher of *USA TODAY* for eight years. And now as CEO of the Newspaper Association of America.

Now, before you brace yourselves and start expecting to have to listen to stories about how far I walked to school in the snow as a child . . . Let me assure you my point is only this . . . You won't have to fight your way in. Up, yes! In, no! Or no more than any guy looking for a job.

But, as your careers progress, you will have your encounters with those walking anachronisms that still populate too much of American business, education, government, media, advertising and even in non profit.

You will encounter the remnants of systematized in-equities . . . where the leaders of the organization are totally out of sync with those who populate it. Where differences are not valued.

We're also still a culture that pays more attention to Marcia Clark's hair and divorce than it does to her considerable legal skills.

You will encounter those who will criticize the choices you make in your life . . . too much ambition . . . works too hard . . . she doesn't have a life . . . who will too quickly say "that you can't have it all."

Well, I've chosen both . . . and even though there are days when I question my sanity, I wouldn't change it for a moment.

I cherish my home life . . . my husband . . . (in fact, today is our 13th wedding anniversary) and my young children.

To me there is no greater sound in the world than to walk in the door and hear someone say . . . "hi mom" and to get a hug. But, I also cherish my work.

High expectations and accomplishments on the job have always held a deep meaning for me . . . it's just part of who I am. I've been lucky, yes. But, I've also earned it. I made my choices. And I've never regretted them.

And, you will make your choices . . . and whatever they are, I believe you will be the generation to sweep away the preconceptions . . . of what's right and wrong for women . . . and reposition the argument to where it should be . . . what's right and wrong for you.

In the workplace, I believe you will have the chance . . . much more than the generations before you . . . to succeed on your merits.

Now, I'm the first to admit that I've been predicting equality in the work place for 20 years now . . . and some of my most confident predictions have yet to come true.

But, I think change is finally at hand. Just look at the numbers . . . over 35 percent of MBA degrees today go to women . . . over 40 percent of CPA's are women. I guess somebody forgot to tell these people that girls can't do math.

And for those who want to strike out on their own . . . woman-owned businesses are growing 50 percent faster than male-owned businesses. Clearly . . . there's something going on here.

I believe the sheer power of your presence is going to make gender the irrelevancy that it should have been long . . . long ago . . . with the pressing career and life issues evening out on both sides of the great chromosomal divide. And that's just as true whether your path takes you to work, home or both.

Given that . . . I'd like to talk with you about what I see as the prime expectation in this new world of high opportunity and high-uncertainty. And that is the expectation for individual leadership.

Leadership is the defining issue . . . for individuals, organizations, and non profits . . . and any other field of endeavor . . . as we round the turn toward the new millennium. But we must redefine the word "leadership" . . . pound on it a bit to fit in some new requisites. After all . . . what are leaders? and what can they really do?

Except for *Jeopardy*'s Alex Trebeck . . . nobody has all the answers.

Even our most revered leaders are . . . at the end of the day . . . just people . . . created of the same mix of triumph and foible as everyone else. Leadership is a condition . . . a situation . . . a response . . . a responsibility . . . a demand . . . a place in time . . . an outlook. It's all of that . . . and even more . . . it's a game that we all get to play. It's a game we all must play.

Say good-bye to revering the boss . . . the head man . . . the top dog . . . *numero uno* . . . the *cappo-de-tutti-capo* . . . the keeper of all knowledge . . . and dispenser of all wisdom. Leadership in the world you are about to enter is much more egalitarian than all that.

With events spinning at warp speed . . . with old structures collapsing on a world scale . . . with new ones rising to take their place . . . detailed, step-by-step instructions from a higher authority . . . like time itself . . . is a luxury . . . meaning that all of us . . . every single one of us in any organization . . . public, private or social . . . should expect to contribute our own special, unique leadership.

The power behind today's structures is the people that populate them . . . the white hot core of brains, guts, drive and experience that combine in the alchemy of achievement. Brains, guts, drive, and experience . . . a useful definition, I think for leadership. Missing only one ingredient . . . faith. Others might pick commitment.

Real leadership takes more than just commitment . . . which is really simple determination gussied up in the new-speak of empowerment. Real leadership to me has always been an act of faith. Faith in yourself . . . the ability to project yourself into the role of leader.

The toughest part of fulfilling the coming leadership demands is to latch on to the belief . . . to have faith . . . in your personal leadership rights and responsibilities . . . fervently . . . absolutely . . . without question. And that can be a stretch for some women . . . especially those who still believe that leadership means you have to walk like John Wayne, talk like James Earl Jones and have the fiery presence of Margaret Thatcher.

There are other models . . . Mother Theresa . . . serene, but with a will of granite. And from my own line of work . . . the *Washington Post*'s very courageous Katherine Graham. Or, the First Lady . . . Hillary Rodham Clinton. But, I promised at the start that I wouldn't be dealing in absolutes about your future.

But, I can . . . based on finding my own way along that path . . . point out a few of leadership's mile markers. Some are obvious . . . like a reasonable level of intelligence . . . although effective leaders don't have to flash their MENSA cards, but values like perception, judgment, quick thinking, and flexibility absolutely all count. Along with honesty . . . a work ethic . . . drive . . . the ability to work on a team . . . a tolerance for ambiguity and risk.

But let me skip over all that . . . and look at the one element I think will set apart the true leader. Psychologist Ellen Langer calls it "mindfulness." Langer defines mindfulness as the ability to pay attention to the essence and potential of things rather than be blinded and inhibited by the categories applied to them.

That has a special meaning, I think for women, who for too long have, in fact, been blinded to possibilities . . . and confined to categories. Because the ability to see the essence of a situation is innate . . . certainly not science . . . clearly more than art . . . perhaps a fusion of gifted ability and life experience.

But I believe . . . I've actually seen it in action . . . that such abilities can also be learned. It's the ability to force yourself to think outside the lines . . . especially when someone has drawn those lines for you. To look at every problem totally unfettered by the past . . . especially past success.

Leadership is . . . it's the ability to see what everyone else sees . . . but think what nobody else has thought.

So, let me close today with an observation and a request.

My observation is that you . . . graduates of St. Mary's . . . like the many thousands of others from colleges and universities all across the country . . . are entering a world that is at the same time more expansive in its opportunity . . . and more daunting in its uncertainties . . . than the generations before you could have dreamed.

And my request is this. Use those opportunities . . . and use those uncertainties to build yourselves into the model of a 21st century leader. Look deeply into the essence of each situation you encounter . . . don't take anything for granted. Don't be blinded by the presumptions of others. Don't be categorized by assigned roles. Stand up for what you believe in. And, create from that a unique potential . . . fashioned from the very special stuff of who you are . . . what you've learned . . . where you've been . . . what your values are . . . what you want . . . and how you can grow.

It's your life!! It's your time!! Make the most of both.

Thank you . . . best wishes . . . and good luck.

WHEN COMMUNITIES FLOURISH[3]
HILLARY RODHAM CLINTON

First Lady of the United States; born Chicago, IL, 1947; B.A., Wellesley College, 1969; J.D., Yale University, 1973; attorney for Children's Defense Fund, 1973–74; assistant professor of law, University of Arkansas, 1974–77; Partner, Rose Law Firm, Little Rock, AR, 1977–   ; Head of Rural Health Advisory Committee, AK, 1979–80; Head of Task Force on National Health Care Reform; Outstanding Person of theYear, Phi Delta Kappa; honorary President, Girl Scouts of America.

Editors' introduction: On September 5, 1995, Hillary Rodham Clinton addressed the United Nations Fourth World Conference on Women, in Beijing, China, the largest gathering of its kind. "I have very high hopes that this will not be just a lot of talk," Clinton said, "but will enable us to learn from one another." Patrick E. Tyler reported that "the 10-day meeting of more than 4,000 government delegates will seek to produce a 'platform for action' to influence the policies of world governments on women's rights in health, education, business, and politics." Clinton spoke "more forcefully on human rights than any American dignitary has on Chinese soil" (*New York Times*, Sept. 5 and 6, 1995). "The pointed address to delegates evoked cheers, applause, and pounding on tables." "To me," Clinton explained, "it was important to express how I felt and to do so as clearly as I could." The *Chicago Tribune* (Sept. 5, 1995) found that Clinton's "veiled attack

[3]Delivered at the United Nations World Conference on Women, on September 5, 1995.

on human rights in China sparked jubilation among rights activists." The *Detroit News & Free Press* (Sept. 6, 1995) praised Clinton's "championing of women's rights in the context of human rights." The *Boston Globe* (Sept. 7, 1995) editorialized that Clinton's remarks were "skillfully pointed without provoking retaliations from the Chinese communist regime." The *New York Times* (Sept. 6, 1995) reviewer wrote: "Clinton's unapologetic affirmation of American values is a departure from the bland and euphemistic rhetoric of other recent United States diplomatic visitors to Beijing." Clinton's speech was published in *Congressional Record* (Sept. 5,1995) and *Vital Speeches* (Oct. 1, 1995).

Hillary Rodham Clinton's speech: Mrs. Mongella, Under Secretary Kittani, distinguished delegates and guests:

I would like to thank the Secretary General of the United Nations for inviting me to be part of the United Nations Fourth World Conference on Women. This is truly a celebration—a celebration of the contributions women make in every aspect of life: in the home, on the job, in their communities, as mothers, wives, sisters, daughters, learners, workers, citizens and leaders.

It is also a coming together, much the way women come together every day in every country.

We come together in fields and in factories. In village markets and supermarkets. In living rooms and board rooms.

Whether it is while playing with our children in the park, or washing clothes in a river, or taking a break at the office water cooler, we come together and talk about our aspirations and concerns. And time and again, our talk turns to our children and our families. However different we may be, there is far more that unites us than divides us. We share a common future. And we are here to find common ground so that we may help bring new dignity and respect to women and girls all over the world—and in so doing, bring new strength and stability to families as well.

By gathering in Beijing, we are focusing world attention on issues that matter most in the lives of women and their families: access to education, health care, jobs and credit, the chance to enjoy basic legal and human rights and participate fully in the political life of their countries.

There are some who question the reason for this conference.

Let them listen to the voices of women in their homes, neighborhoods, and workplaces.

There are some who wonder whether the lives of women and girls matter to economic and political progress around the globe.

Let them look at the women gathered here and at Huairou— the homemakers, nurses, teachers, lawyers, policymakers, and women who run their own businesses.

It is conferences like this that compel governments and people everywhere to listen, look and face the world's most pressing problems.

Wasn't it after the women's conference in Nairobi ten years ago that the world focused for the first time on the crisis of domestic violence?

Earlier today, I participated in a World Health Organization forum, where government officials, NGOs, and individual citizens are working on ways to address the health problems of women and girls.

Tomorrow, I will attend a gathering of the United Nations Development Fund for Women. There, the discussion will focus on local—and highly successful—programs that give hardworking women access to credit so they can improve their own lives and the lives of their families.

What we are learning around the world is that if women are healthy and educated, their families will flourish. If women are free from violence, their families will flourish. If women have a chance to work and earn as full and equal partners in society, their families will flourish.

And when families flourish, communities and nations will flourish.

That is why every woman, every man, every child, every family, and every nation on our planet has a stake in the discussion that takes place here.

Over the past 25 years, I have worked persistently on issues relating to women, children and families. Over the past two-and-a-half years, I have had the opportunity to learn more about the challenges facing women in my own country and around the world.

I have met new mothers in Jojakarta, Indonesia, who come together regularly in their village to discuss nutrition, family planning, and baby care.

I have met working parents in Denmark who talk about the comfort they feel in knowing that their children can be cared for in creative, safe, and nurturing after-school centers.

I have met women in South Africa who helped lead the struggle to end apartheid and are now helping build a new democracy.

I have met with the leading women of the Western Hemisphere who are working every day to promote literacy and better health care for the children of their countries.

I have met women in India and Bangladesh who are taking out small loans to buy milk cows, rickshaws, thread and other materials to create a livelihood for themselves and their families.

I have met doctors and nurses in Belarus and Ukraine who are trying to keep children alive in the aftermath of Chernobyl.

The great challenge of this Conference is to give voice to women everywhere whose experiences go unnoticed, whose words go unheard.

Women comprise more than half the world's population. Women are 70% percent of the world's poor, and two-thirds of those who are not taught to read and write.

Women are the primary caretakers for most of the world's children and elderly. Yet much of the work we do is not valued—not by economists, not by historians, not by popular culture, not by government leaders.

At this very moment, as we sit here, women around the world are giving birth, raising children, cooking meals, washing clothes, cleaning houses, planting crops, working on assembly lines, running companies, and running countries.

Women also are dying from diseases that should have been prevented or treated; they are watching their children succumb to malnutrition caused by poverty and economic deprivation; they are being denied the right to go to school by their own fathers and brothers; they are being forced into prostitution, and they are being barred from the bank lending office and banned from the ballot box.

Those of us who have the opportunity to be here have the responsibility to speak for those who could not.

As an American, I want to speak up for women in my own country—women who are raising children on the minimum wage, women who can't afford health care or child care, women whose lives are threatened by violence, including violence in their own homes.

I want to speak up for mothers who are fighting for good schools, safe neighborhoods, clean air and clean airwaves; for older women, some of them widows, who have raised their families and now find that their skills and life experiences are not valued in the workplace; for women who are working all night as nurses, hotel clerks, and fast food cooks so that they can be at home during the day with their kids; and for women everywhere who simply don't have time to do everything they are called upon to do each day.

Speaking to you today, I speak for them, just as each of us speaks for women around the world who are denied the chance to go to school, or see a doctor, or own property, or have a say about the direction of their lives, simply because they are women. The truth is that most women around the world work both inside and outside the home, usually by necessity.

We need to understand that there is no formula for how women should lead their lives.

That is why we must respect the choices that each woman makes for herself and her family. Every woman deserves the chance to realize her God-given potential.

We also must recognize that women will never gain full dignity until their human rights are respected and protected.

Our goals for this Conference, to strengthen families and societies by empowering women to take greater control over their own destinies, cannot be fully achieved unless all governments—here and around the world—accept their responsibility to protect and promote internationally recognized human rights.

The international community has long acknowledged and recently affirmed at Vienna—that both women and men are entitled to a range of protections and personal freedoms, from the right of personal security to the right to determine freely the number and spacing of the children they bear.

No one should be forced to remain silent for fear of religious or political persecution, arrest, abuse or torture.

Tragically, women are most often the ones whose human rights are violated.

Even in the late 20th century, the rape of women continues to be used as an instrument of armed conflict. Women and children make up a large majority of the world's refugees. When women are excluded from the political process, they become even more vulnerable to abuse.

I believe that, on the eve of a new millennium, it is time to break our silence. It is time for us to say here in Beijing, and the world to hear, that it is no longer acceptable to discuss women's rights as separate from human rights.

These abuses have continued because, for too long, the history of women has been a history of silence. Even today, there are those who are trying to silence our words.

The voices of this conference and of the women at Huairou must be heard loud and clear:

It is a violation of human rights when babies are denied food, or drowned, or suffocated, or their spines broken, simply because they are born girls.

It is a violation of human rights when women and girls are sold into the slavery of prostitution.

It is a violation of human rights when women are doused with gasoline, set on fire and burned to death because their marriage dowries are deemed too small.

It is a violation of human rights when individual women are raped in their own communities and when thousands of women are subjected to rape as a tactic or prize of war.

It is a violation of human rights when a leading cause of death worldwide among women ages 14 to 44 is the violence they are subjected to in their own homes.

It is a violation of human rights when young girls are brutalized by the painful and degrading practice of genital mutilation.

It is a violation of human rights when women are denied the right to plan their own families, and that includes being forced to have abortions or being sterilized against their will.

If there is one message that echoes forth from this conference, it is that human rights are women's rights and women's rights are human rights. Let us not forget that among those rights are the right to speak freely—and the right to be heard.

Women must enjoy the right to participate fully in the social and political lives of their countries if we want freedom and democracy to thrive and endure.

It is indefensible that many women in nongovernmental organizations who wished to participate in this conference have not been able to attend—or have been prohibited from fully taking part.

Let me be clear. Freedom means the right of people to assemble, organize, and debate openly. It means respecting the views of those who may disagree with the views of their governments.

It means not taking citizens away from their loved ones and jailing them, mistreating them, or denying them their freedom or dignity because of the peaceful expression of their ideas and opinions.

In my country, we recently celebrated the 75th anniversary of women's suffrage. It took 150 years after the signing of our Declaration of Independence for women to win the right to vote.

It took 72 years of organized struggle on the part of many courageous women and men. It was one of America's most divisive philosophical wars. But it was also a bloodless war. Suffrage was achieved without a shot being fired.

We have also been reminded, in V-J Day observances last weekend, of the good that comes when men and women join together to combat the forces of tyranny and build a better world.

We have seen peace prevail in most places for a half century. We have avoided another world war.

But we have not solved older, deeply-rooted problems that continue to diminish the potential of half the world's population.

Now it is time to act on behalf of women everywhere.

If we take bold steps to better the lives of women, we will be taking bold steps to better the lives of children and families too.

Families rely on mothers and wives for emotional support and care; families rely on women for labor in the home; and increasingly, families rely on women for income needed to raise healthy children and care for other relatives.

As long as discrimination and inequities remain so commonplace around the world—as long as girls and women are valued less, fed less, fed last, overworked, underpaid, not schooled, and subjected to violence in and out of their homes—the potential of the human family to create a peaceful, prosperous world will not be realized.

Let this Conference be our—and the world's—call to action.

And let us heed the call so that we can create a world in which every woman is treated with respect and dignity, every boy and girl is loved and cared for equally, and every family has the hope of a strong and stable future.

Thank you very much.

God's blessings on you, your work, and all who will benefit from it.

VI. FUNCTION AND IMPACT OF MEDIA

AS OLD GODS FALTER[1]
WILLIAM F. WOO

Editor, St. Louis Post-Dispatch,*1986–   ; born Shanghai, China, 1938; A.B., University of Kansas; reporter,* Kansas City Star, *1957–62; Missouri Medal of Honor, University of Missouri, 1991; Chair of Ethics Committee, the American Society of Newspaper (ASNE) Editors.*

Editors' introduction: Editor William F. Woo gave this lecture, entitled, "As Old Gods Falter: Public Journalism and The Tradition of Detachment," as the 30th in the *Press-Enterprise* Series at Riverside, California, February 13, 1995. The series was begun in 1966 in cooperation with the University of California, Riverside, and has "become a nationally known forum for important issues in American journalism." Previous speakers were David Broder, George Will, James Reston, Tom Wicker, and Katharine Graham (Mark Petix, *Press-Enterprise,* Feb. 12, 1995). Chair Howard H. (Tim) Hays explained that "the intent of the series is to bring to the university each year someone of exceptional achievement in journalism to further the interest of both the university community and the general community in journalism."

Art Charity judged Woo to be "the rare journalist who has ventured into the as-yet-unfilled niche of truly engaged critic: He's sympathetic to public journalism's aims but suspicious of its practices" (*Quill,* Jan./Feb. 1996). While public journalism has been described as "boosterism" by the *New York Times,* David "Buzz" Merritt, Jr., editor of the *Wichita Eagle* advised that "it is not smart or correct for community papers to follow the lead of the big papers. One size does not fit all. . . . We need a healthy debate" (Mark Petix, *Press-Enterprise*, Feb. 20, 1995).

Woo read his address in the theater at the university, to more than 250 citizens of the community along with journalists, students, and faculty. The speech was the event of the evening and

[1]Delivered at the University of California, Riverside, CA, February 13, 1995, at 8:15.

recorded for broadcast over KUCR. Woo related to the editors of this volume how he "attempted to provide a much needed critical analysis for the emerging theory of public journalism." His strategy was to "draw heavily on history of the tradition of detachment, analyze the penance of public journalism, and raise a number of pointed questions about the practice." Woo found the response to his address to be very favorable. "There were many questions from the audience, and I have received numerous invitations to appear at journalism forums to discuss journalism."

William F. Woo's speech: First, I must thank Tim Hays and *The Press-Enterprise* and also the University of California at Riverside for the honor of being invited here tonight. I need to thank them, too, for the confidence that I can speak adequately about our profession, which remains noble and capacious in its possibilities but which also is deeply troubled.

Under these same auspices four years ago, David Broder, the finest political reporter of this or perhaps any time, made a remarkable confession. For 30 years, he said, "we reported everything that was happening in American politics—except that it was collapsing." Fewer people were voting; more and more people were saying they were disgusted with politics.

As Broder saw it, journalists and consultants had become the permanent part of the political establishment, unlike candidates, who came and went. The political information that the American public acquired came from people who disclaimed any responsibility for the outcome of elections.

David Broder had a suggestion. We need, he said, to distance ourselves from the people we write about—the politicians and consultants—and move closer to the people we write for—the voters and potential voters. Journalists had assumed that the campaigns belonged to the candidates. Henceforth, we should understand that they belong to the voters.

This was revolutionary. Not many people were asserting such things back then. You could say that David Broder was a kind of John the Baptist crying in the wilderness. Let the people set the agenda. Find out what they want and compel the candidates to respond.

As for the candidates? David Broder's answer was this: "Obviously, we can't ignore what the candidates choose to do and say. But when they're talking about things that are irrelevant to the voters' concerns, we don't have to give it the same coverage we do when they are addressing what we know to be very much on the voters' minds."

Now this was only an extension of past practice, but formerly it had been the voters' hopes and fears that had been given short shrift. That was wrong, but was the proper corrective to turn the table on the candidates?

Perhaps so, but as I read those words the traffic light at the corner, where revolution intersects tradition, turned yellow. For I thought of the candidate with a vision, one who went well beyond what most people were thinking about. But if we were convinced we already knew what really was on the public's mind, what would be our coverage? And what would become of the vision?

David Broder's prescription is at the heart of what we now know as public journalism. He was not alone in thinking about these things in 1991. A few people here and there were also giving this concept some serious consideration.

But Broder's voice was powerful, and what he had to say became a rallying cry for the new idea, towards which converts eagerly flocked. Earlier I referred to Broder as a kind of John the Baptist and now I use the word "converts."

The allusions to religion are self-conscious, but I am by no means the first to draw the connection. "The Gospel of Public Journalism" was the title of a recent article in the *American Journalism Review*, which described the concept as "the hottest secular religion in the news business."

Those in its service have been called evangelists or zealots or prophets. The witty Roy Peter Clark of the Poynter Institute refers to Jay Rosen, director of the Project on Public Life and the Press at New York University, and surely the Apostle Paul of the movement, as a wise man from the East.

New religions rise when old ones wither or die, when the faith grows frail and tired gods falter. In a perceptive speech back in 1990, Philip Meyer of the University of North Carolina noted that the old order was changing, and he predicted "a period of moral confusion as the players change and as the media grope for a new ethic."

No one can doubt that we journalists are now deeply in the midst of moral confusion. It would be astonishing, actually, if this were not so.

Everywhere you look there is evidence of the adversity confronting newspapers, or dizzying social and technological changes about which we have yet to decide whether they are opportunities or perils or both. As my Chinese forebears would say, we live in interesting times.

Let me sketch in our difficulties. Since 1950, daily circulation has been declining as a percentage of population. The September ABC figures showed that every one of America's 15 largest newspapers lost daily readers—more than a quarter million in all. Think of it as if the *Seattle Times* suddenly had ceased to exist.

Although the economy has grown significantly in the past five years, advertising revenues are still below those of 1989. The Yellow Pages, direct mail and specialty catalogs, alternate delivery systems—these have joined broadcast and billboards to chew away at our franchise.

The five-year Veronis, Suhler report on the communications industry tells us that in 1994 the average American spent 9 hours and 3 minutes a day involved with media—watching TV, listening to the radio or recorded music, reading newspapers or magazines, playing video games, doing consumer transactions over the computer and so forth.

Of those 9 hours, fewer than 28 minutes were spent on newspapers; and that figure is going steadily down. More than four hours were spent on television.

We sink in the polls, in terms of the public's confidence, appreciation and esteem.

As I said, it would be astonishing if there were not confusion and a skepticism about the continued legitimacy of the old order. Thinking of journalists at a conference put on by the Nieman Foundation last year, Lawrence K. Grossman, the former president of NBC and PBS, was reminded of a description of the Greek chorus: "[O]ld citizens full of their proverbial wisdom and hopelessness."

Public journalism is not the only response to our new circumstances. As faith and confidence are challenged, other gods have appeared.

Sensationalism, the tabloidization of the news, is one of them. Indiscretions, scandals, the president's underwear, the Bobbitts, Tonya Harding, O. J. Simpson—we seem powerless to get them off the front pages.

We hear that this is what the people want; and moreover that such stories actually involve matters of importance—fitness to hold public office, spousal abuse, perceptions of race and on. Our papers have become edited by the supermarket tabloids, which set the agenda in subject and detail, in the naming of rape victims.

The new media is another response. Increasingly, we talk of being in the information business, not the news business. More than 50 newspapers have on-line services and more than 600 have audiotext. Every day another paper invests in Virtual Journalism.

The change movement that is sweeping through newsrooms is still another. Some 40 editors showed up for the September meeting of the ASNE Change Committee in Minneapolis, an unprecedented attendance for such meetings. "Change is the name of the game," says Tim McGuire, the committee's chair.

Transactional change, transformational change, change facilitator: Get to know the language. Get to know the new structures: the newsroom without walls, the beats with names like hunters and gatherers (instead of county cops or city hall)—a unit, as in Dayton, responsible for covering Private Life and another responsible for covering Real Life.

If this seems odd, remember that if we do not evolve, we shall surely perish. What changes to make? What values to keep? These are the questions.

And then there is public journalism, the hot new secular religion. Is this our salvation? Nobody, surely, is ready to make so sweeping a claim. In fact, the proponents of public journalism talk of it as a work in progress.

Some examples of public journalism are impressive, and I am intrigued by what may lie down that road, beyond the bend. I am greatly respectful of the leading thinkers and practitioners; people like Jay Rosen, Buzz Merritt, Phil Meyer, Frank Denton, among others. Improving democracy is a grand undertaking.

And yet, I am unsettled by what I see. So tonight, I would like to hold public journalism up to the light and turn it around and look more carefully at the outlines and the shadows.

What is public journalism? David Broder had it in a nutshell: To move ourselves closer to the people we write for.

Jay Rosen offered an excellent conceptual description at the American Press Institute last June. The distinction between traditional journalism and public journalism, Rosen declared, is that the former is worried abut getting the separations right, whereas the latter is about trying to get the connections right.

Traditional journalism is journalism that is detached, that sees its mission in keeping itself separate from the institutions it reports on; in keeping facts separate from values, news from editorial.

Public journalism is journalism that is attached, that connects press and politics, news product and business function, journalists and the community. The public journalist goes beyond merely covering politics to play a positive role in making the community's politics "go well."

Here is Rosen's mission statement: "Traditional journalism seeks to 'inform the public' and act as a 'watchdog' over government. Public journalism tries to strengthen the community's capacity to recognize itself, converse well, and make choices."

From this and similar ideas, many flowers have bloomed. The most celebrated among them—The *Wichita Eagle's* voters project in 1992 and The *Charlotte Observer's* program that same year to focus on an election agenda set by the readers—by now are familiar to most journalists.

These and other widely publicized projects are only the top of the iceberg. The *American Journalism Review* reported last September that 171 newspapers were working with Rosen's Project on Public Life and the Press and that 95 initiatives in public journalism were underway.

From this idea, too, assumptions flow that challenge the most deeply held principles of traditional journalism: detachment, objectivity, the belief that editors are the final judges over what is news. It also has led to some provocative redefinitions of journalism.

"If democracy is to have a post-modern expression," Rosen has written, "the press must come to see itself as a construction site, where worlds are made and need to be made well."

Buzz Merritt says that journalists should define themselves not as being in the information or watchdog business but in the business of public life, the business of democracy.

Rick Thames, the editor in charge of the *Charlotte Observer's* Citizens Agenda project, says that "We weren't just a newspaper anymore; we were the electorate." That is a startling transformation if you think about it.

Some interesting academic work validates the premise of public journalism.

Neuman, Just and Crigler, the authors of "Common Knowledge: News and the Construction of Political Meaning," found a critical disjuncture between what the media tell people is important. For example, people tune out politics because they feel powerless.

They found, too, that traditional journalism often reinforces the sense of powerlessness by stressing the complexity of issues, a practice we have valued—mistakenly, it might appear—as in-depth reporting. But the authors discovered that people are enthusiastic about information that helps them take control of public events, and they recommended that journalists incorporate an element of civic action into their stories.

Many public journalism projects have been directed at improving the electoral process. As one editor was quoted in *AJR*, "I'd rather increase voter turnout 10 percent than win a Pulitzer."

This past election, papers from coast to coast experimented with public journalism. Broadcast, too, was involved. NPR enlisted nearly 90 of its member stations to engage the public in its coverage of the election. In several cities such as Boston, Dallas and Seattle, public broadcasting worked hand in hand with newspapers.

So all over America the press was attached to readers as never before. Surveys, focus groups, town meetings, citizen advisory boards—all these and more came into play as the press attempted to move closer to the voters and farther away from the candidates and their agendas and horse races.

Furthermore, what would work with politics should also work with other civic endeavors. And so across the landscape public journalism moved into many phases of community life.

In Dayton, Ohio, the paper buys pizzas to get people together to talk about youth violence and other urgent issues. In Spokane, Washington, the paper has eliminated the position of editorial page editor and has created, instead, two interactive editors to help citizens get their opinions into the paper.

The *Wisconsin State Journal* in Madison has been working with broadcast partners for several years on a project called We the People. It sponsors town hall meetings and is now moving into an action-oriented jobs program for the city.

In Portland, Maine, the newspaper organized a meeting with the governor, legislative leaders and business and labor officials to resolve an impasse on workers' compensation. In Bremerton, Washington, *The Sun* teamed up with banking and real estate interests to combine their muscle to force the county commission to place a bond issue for open space on the ballot.

Does it work? It is too soon to tell, although there are impressive success stories. Increases in voter turnout have been registered, in the case of Charlotte by more than 30 percent. The *Akron Beacon-Journal's* public journalism project to help the community deal with racial division won the Pulitzer Prize for Public Service. Measured by citizen interest and participation, public journalism clearly catches community interest.

Voter turnout last November was up 2.2 percent over the 1990 midterm election. Was that because of public journalism or Rush Limbaugh or the Republican landslide—or some combination of the three? In any case, it is promising evidence.

So far, public journalism has done little to stem the tide in circulation losses across America. But here, too, we need to be patient.

In every example of public journalism the foremost principle has been that the newspaper and its journalists can no longer remain detached; that they must be involved and activists. The underlying assumption is that through community or democratic action, a newspaper may recapture the worthiness of purpose and relevance that traditional, detached journalism has frittered away—and also, as we shall see, replenish its depleted revenue stream.

Editors sit on public boards or commissions or action committees. Newspapers are becoming the conveners of their community, the master of ceremonies of the new democracy. Journalists no longer serve or inform the electorate; they become it.

So I would turn now to an examination of the premise of public journalism and to some specific concerns I have about the practice, concerns that may or may not be well grounded. As they say, this is a work in progress.

Proponents of public journalism hold that traditions such as detachment or objectivity essentially are creations of market conditions. Hence, as those conditions change, these traditions and values can be discarded or, at the least, reexamined. Evolving economic circumstances deprive them of any claim to immutability.

Thus in his speech five years ago, Phil Meyer argued that to attract advertising, newspaper needed to be credible, trusted institutions. "That is the economic basis for the traditional separation of business and editorial sides on a newspaper," he said.

Jay Rosen, elaborating on the idea in his API presentation, went on to say that the production of the credibility, demanded by advertisers, was the job of the newsroom. "The logical way to do the job was to grant independence to the editorial voice," he said. "Thus came the professional ethic of objectivity, distance and detachment."

A fundamental assumption of public journalism, then, is that objectivity and detachment are accommodations to specific business requirements that developed long ago. If they have no more significant history than that, we are not losing anything essential when we clear them out to make way for the connected, undetached journalism.

For after all, business circumstances change. Advertisers no longer are dependent on newspapers to reach their audiences. The credibility that detachment or independence brought no longer sustains newspapers, no longer creates value. Something else, as the proponents say, is needed to take its place.

Now when it comes to journalism, I have trouble with what scientists refer to as a general theory, that is, one—such as Einstein's theory of relativity—that governs all aspects of a particular phenomenon.

I prefer an idea such as the one expressed in 1925 by Robert Park, in his essay on the natural history of the newspaper, in which he wrote: "The newspaper, like the modern city, is not wholly a rational product. No one sought to make it just what it is."

That is, while I accept that the desire to accommodate advertisers furthered the ideal of detachment, I cannot believe that this explains it all. Were there not other factors?

Michael Schudson, the sociologist, turned his doctoral dissertation into an interesting book called "Discovering the News," in which he examined why journalists believe they needed to be objective. Objectivity in journalism is more than just a claim to what is reliable, he wrote: "It is also a moral philosophy, a declaration of what kind of thinking one should engage in, in making moral decisions."

Reading Schudson, you can trace the concept of objectivity, if not its articulation, back to the introduction of the penny press in the 1830s, when newspapers began to break free of their partisan moorings and to report the "facts" of a wide range of activities in American life. As journalists became better educated, their interest in facts, accuracy and authoritativeness increased.

Journalists were not insulated from other cultural currents, the movement toward a realist literature, for example. And in the early decades of the twentieth century, they were not exempted from the general decline in faith in democracy and the fear of encroaching unreason. Objectivity became a refuge from doubt and drift. It was a safe harbor in another period of moral confusion.

In her book, "Journalistic Standards in Nineteenth Century America," Hazel Dicken-Garcia points out how critics of the press after 1850 fastened on the subservience of newspapers to advertising, one of them describing the advertisement desk as "the most insidious to the fair fame of journalism."

She relates how editors such as E. L. Godkin in the 1860s advocated the separation of news and "expository" departments. The press commentary in those days saw the separation of news and editorial as essential.

These views, of course, coincide with the beginning of newspapers' dependence on such mass advertisers as department stores. But editors did not see their task as making newspapers safe for advertising. Quite the opposite, they wanted to preserve them from the corrupting effects of commerce.

If you look, as did Stephen Allen Banning of the University of Missouri School of Journalism, at the minutes of the Missouri Press Association in the 1860s and 1870s, what do you find the editors talking about? Those new fangled department stores back East? No. They talked of standards, principles and values.

They talked of journalism's high mission, of truth, of ethics, of dealing with facts—of an editor's responsibility to remain faithful to his own convictions and duty, which is a way of saying, to be detached. And they talked about content: "Give the substance," said William F. Switzler in his address to the association in 1876.

My point in all of this is not to discredit any challenge to the traditions of detachment or objectivity. We all know the bizarre lengths to which these can be carried; and it may well be that they are related to our problems.

My purpose has been to show that these values have long histories, they reflect how journalists have struggled to confront the circumstances of their eras. They have become part of a moral philosophy.

In short, they are an important heritage. To deny them, we must deal with more than a theory based on the exigencies of the commercial life of American newspapers at a particular moment. Before we set them aside, before we declare them obsolete and rush on to something else, we need to understand carefully what we are throwing out. We need a more persuasive argument.

Proponents of public journalism assure us that it is compatible with objectivity and other traditional values. But as a practical matter, can a paper objectively report on a burning community issue when the editor sits on the commission that is promoting a particular point of view on the matter?

If people see that a paper has a vested interest in one issue, will they be more likely to believe it has vested interests everywhere? Does this still matter, particularly since we are being given to understand that the passing of an antique business has liberated credibility from the chains of detachment?

What about some other issues? What about content?

"Why is it that the Prophets of Journalism never seem to talk about the news?" asked Tom Koch in an article last May in *Quill*. Koch is coordinator for computer-assisted journalism at the European Journalism Center, and he had attended a conference on journalism and society at the Poynter Institute, where Jay Rosen, among others, was a speaker.

"They worry," Koch went on, "about the ideals of service, community roles, First Amendment privileges or challenges, journalism-as-business, and the industry's relation to society, but not about what concerns reporters, city editors, and news librarians: the content of the stories that become the product which newspapers, magazines, and broadcast stations present to the world."

Koch told of confronting an academic advocate of public journalism, a department head, in fact, and asking, "What about news? When are you folk going to talk about what's in the stories which are the news?"

Now the lateness of the hour may have had something to do with this exchange. Many of us are not at our best when braced close to midnight after the rigors of conference and post-conference participation. But this was the response Koch got: "You can't create a theory of news based on stories, on story content. It would be very hard to do."

Here is another issue to think about. At an ASNE convention session last year featuring the wisdom of three old heads, Gene Roberts was asked about the homogeneity of newspapers. Was chain journalism the culprit?

No, Roberts replied. If there was homogeneity, chains such as Gannett and Knight-Ridder had probably less to do with it than the fact that editors all go to the same meetings.

That is, we engage in group-think. We hear the same speakers, wherever our conferences or seminars happen to be. We go through the same interactive exercises with the same facilitators. We hire the same consultants, receive the same answers, buy into the same assumptions that are based on the same interpretations of the same data.

Recall now that the Center for Public Life and the Press last fall was working with 171 news organizations. The potential for group-think on a massive scale is obvious. Should we worry about this? Perhaps we are all sufficiently independent-minded as to make the concern needless.

One of the most admirable qualities of public journalism is its focus on citizen participation, particularly in voting. Yet I am concerned that we are redefining the people we write for, from readers to voters or citizens.

We know that large numbers of people who buy our papers do not vote, do not participate. More than 60 percent of those eligible to vote last November did not. The sociologist Herbert Gans finds that the strongest feature of the political activity among middle Americans is something he calls "organizational avoidance"—a phenomenon that increases the more people disperse to the suburbs, which, of course, is where our readers are going.

But we also know that citizen participation and voting increase as the socioeconomic and educational scale goes upward. I think about the possibility of developing an elitism, in which the nonvoter, the non-participator, becomes not merely a second-class citizen but also a second-class reader.

When the lion lies down with the lamb, when the editor and the real estate broker and the banker and the elected official form a team, whose ethics, whose culture prevails? Much of what is commonplace in business or politics, many of the social conventions that make the wheels of progress go around, the fancy dinners and tickets to the luxury box, are expressly forbidden by our codes of conduct and ethics.

It is not enough to say that our own traditional ethics will prevail when the pinch comes; for when the lions and the lambs gather to decide what issues the community will confront, they will not get very far if one side adopts an attitude that the other perceives as holier-than-thou.

I am talking about cultural conflicts posed by public journalism and how we compose them. If one standard of conduct prevails for the editor, pursuing the high-minded civic objectives defined by the public journalism, does it also prevail for the reporter? We teach by example and we need to think this through.

What about the uses of language and nomenclature? What does it mean to say we are not in the watchdog business but the business of public life? One is precise, the other abstract. When we stop thinking of the people we write for as readers and start thinking of them as citizens, our relationship with them changes. The former is more intimate; the latter, more distant.

I think I know what Jay Rosen means when he says we should be about strengthening a community's capacity. I am much surer about what is meant in the *Post-Dispatch* platform, written in 1907 by the first Joseph Pulitzer, where it says "never tolerate injustice or corruption."

When we use the new jargon of journalism, what actually are we trying to say? Orwell's warning that language and thought tend to corrupt each is still relevant.

We now privatize prisons and public schools. Why not privatize democracy itself? Soon we may be able to say: Tuesday's election is brought to you by the friendly folks at the *Post-Dispatch*; the American Dream Reality—where every home is a castle— and the Foreclosure National Bank—see us for your next auto loan.

What are the implications when profit-seeking newspaper companies, either privately held or publicly owned, declare that they have become the electorate? What if IBM or the Yellow Pages or Bill Gates were to assert themselves as the convener of the community?

Are there legitimate shareholder interests in the commitment of corporate assets on behalf of public policies, when advocacy goes beyond the editorial voice? When candidates are associated with such policies, can these assets represent political contributions? How closely can we skirt the lobbying regulations that govern the formal promotion of public issues before legislative bodies?

Finally, I am concerned about the question of where news and editorial decisions are made. Are they made in the newsroom or at the town hall meeting, within the deliberations of the editorial board or in the place where the editor sups with the civic coalition? (Or in the office of the consultant, where life goes on, no matter whether the circulation rises or falls, whether the community achieves capacity or not?)

Yes, we have been isolated, detached, arrogant, disconnected, narrow in our definitions of what's news and what isn't. We have thrived anaerobically in airless environments.

Damn right that we should listen to the public. But should the consensus at the town meeting automatically become our agenda, not merely in editorial support but in the expenditure of resources that determine what other stories do not get covered?

Proponents of public journalism declare that at the end of the day every newspaper must make its own decisions in light of its own values and principles. Fair enough. But I have yet to hear of a paper that said No to what the citizens wanted when the paper itself mobilized the people, of a paper that said to its community, sorry, the agenda we helped create is not for us after all.

We are, as Phil Meyer warned, in a period of moral confusion. Public journalism has potential to help see us through into a better day. But it poses hard questions for traditions and values that we have held and respected for a long time. I fear that we are abandoning these too easily, letting them go without sufficient critical examination.

Let me conclude with a story.

At Christmas, I read our younger sons a book called "The Polar Express." It is about a boy who goes to the North Pole on Christmas Eve and finds under his tree the next morning a Silver bell from Santa's sleigh.

It rings with the most beautiful sound that he and his sister Sarah have ever heard. But his parents cannot hear it at all. Too bad, they say, the bell is broken. This is how the story ends:

"At one time most of my friends could hear the bell, but as years passed, it fell silent for all of them. Even Sarah found one Christmas that she could no longer hear its sweet sound. Though I've grown old, the bell still rings for me as it does for all who truly believe."

It has been nearly 40 years since I sat down at the *Kansas City Times* to write my first news story. So much has happened since then—so many wonderful changes in our business, but also so many challenges, so much doubt and difficulty, so much noise.

It is hard to hear those old bells ringing for objectivity, detachment, independence, for the courage to print stories that are unpopular and for which there is no consensus.

And yet they ring still, ever faintly in the growing tumult. I hope we listen for them again, before we grow so old and so wise that they no longer matter.

HOLLYWOOD VIOLENCE[2]
ROBERT DOLE

U.S. Senator, Kansas, 1968–1996; born, Russell, KS, 1923; A.B., Washburn Municipal University, Topeka, KS, 1952; LL.B., Washburn Municipal University, 1952; twice wounded and twice decorated for "heroic achievement," World War II; U.S. Senate majority and minority Leader; U.S. House of Representatives, 1960–1968.

Editors' introduction: On May 31, 1995, Senator Bob Dole, at 71, was on the campaign trail for the presidency when he criticized the "entire entertainment industry" for its preoccupation with violence, before a fund-raising dinner of about 600 business leaders and Republican supporters in Los Angeles, California (Bernard Weinraub, *New York Times*, June 1, 1995). Initial response to Dole's speech ranged from "muted to angry." Lara Bergthold, executive director of the Hollywood Women's Political Committee judged the speech to be "unbelievable hypocrisy" (Weinraub, *New York Times*, June 1, 1995). An editorial in the *New York Times* (July 2, 1995) criticized Dole for "pandering to the [political] right." Film critics Gene Siskel and Roger Ebert accused Dole of trying to "make points with the far right" (Marc Sandalow, *San Francisco Chronicle* June 9, 1995).

In a speech in Billings, Montana, the day after Dole's Hollywood speech, Bill Clinton, campaigning for re-election as President, castigated officials who are "only too happy to criticize violence in movies or rap music lyrics, but are stone-cold silent

[2]Delivered in Los Angeles, CA, on May 31, 1995.

about similar right-wing rhetoric" (*Atlanta Constitution*, June 2, 1995). In a town hall meeting in Nashville, Tennessee, on July 10, 1995, Clinton supported use of a computer chip to screen out violent television programs: "Parents can't do it all and they can't do completely without the entertainment media" (White House text). In the United States Senate, on June 28, 1996 (*Congressional Record*), Dole reviewed the debate his speech had helped provoke: "It has been nearly 9 months since I made a speech . . . suggesting that our entertainment industry has a responsibility to look beyond the bottom line and to not pollute our culture and our children. That speech ignited a national discussion . . . which has continued to this day. . . . Tomorrow . . . a delegation of entertainment industry leaders will meet with the congressional Republican leadership . . . and then with President Clinton." Later in 1996, federal legislation approved the computer chip for television sets, giving parents more control of what their children viewed.

Robert Dole's speech: Thank you very much. John, I appreciate that kind introduction. I appreciate all the work that Lod Cook and others have done tonight—Jim Montgomery and many of my friends who are here.

I want to talk about a specific matter tonight. I may not win an Oscar, but I'll talk about it anyway. I want to talk to you tonight about the future of America—about issues of moral importance, matters of social consequence.

Last month, during my announcement tour, I gave voice to concerns held across this country about what is happening to our popular culture. I made what I thought was an obvious point that worries countless American parents: that one of the greatest threats to American family values is the way our popular culture ridicules them. Our music, movies, television and advertising regularly push the limits of decency, bombarding our children with destructive messages of casual violence and even more casual sex. And I concluded that we must hold Hollywood and the entire entertainment industry accountable for putting profit ahead of common decency.

So here I am in California—the home of the entertainment industry and to many of the people who shape our popular culture. And I'm asking for their help. I believe our country is crying out for leaders who will call us as a people to our better nature, not to profit from our weaknesses; who will bring back our confidences in the good, not play on our fears of life's dark corners. This is true for those of us who seek public office. And it is true for those who are blessed with the talent to lead America's vaunted entertainment industry.

Actors and producers, writers and directors, people of talent around the world dream of coming to Hollywood. Because if you are the best, this is where you are. Americans were pioneers in film, and dominate world-wide competition today. The American entertainment industry is at the cutting edge of creative excellence, but also too often the leading edge of a culture becoming dangerously coarse.

I have two goals here tonight. One is to make crystal clear to you the effect this industry has on America's children, in the hope that it will rise to their defense. And the other is to speak more broadly about the corporate executives who hide behind the lofty language of free speech in order to profit from the debasing of America.

There is often heard in Hollywood a kind of "aw shucks" response to attempts to link societal effects with causes in the culture. It's the "we just make the movies people want" response. I'll take that up in a minute. But when they go to work tomorrow, when they sift through competing proposals for their time and their money, when they consider how badly they need the next job, I want the leaders of the entertainment industry to think about the influence they have on America's children.

Let there be no mistake: television and movie screens, boomboxes and headsets are windows on the world for our children. If you are too old or too sophisticated, or too close to the problem, just ask a parent. What to some is art, to our children is a nightly news report on the world outside their limited experiences. What to some is make believe, to them is the "real skinny" on the adult world they are so eager to experience. Kids know firsthand what they see in their families, their schools, their immediate communities. But our popular culture shapes their view of the "real world." Our children believe those paintings in celluloid are reflections of reality. But I don't recognize America in much of what I see.

My voice and the rising voices of millions of other Americans who share this view represent more than the codgy old attempt of one generation to steal the fun of another. A line has been crossed—not just of taste, but of human dignity and decency. It is crossed every time sexual violence is given a catchy tune. When teen suicide is [s]et to an appealing beat. When Hollywood's dream factories turn out nightmares of depravity.

You know what I mean. I mean "Natural Born Killers." "True Romance." Films that revel in mindless violence and loveless sex. I'm talking about groups like "Cannibal Corpse," "Geto Boys" and "2 Live Crew." About a culture business that makes money from "music" extolling the pleasures of raping, torturing, and mutilating women: from "songs" about killing policemen and rejecting law. The mainstreaming of deviancy must come to an end, but it will only stop when the leaders of the entertainment industry recognize and shoulder their responsibility.

But let me be clear: I am not saying that our growing social problems are entirely Hollywood's fault. They are not. People are responsible for their actions. Movies and music do not make children murderers. But a numbing exposure to graphic violence and immorality does steal away innocence, smothering our instinct for outrage. And I think we have reached the point where our popular culture threatens to undermine our character as a nation.

Which brings me to my second point tonight. Our freedom is precious. I have risked my life to defend it, and would do so again. We must always be proud in America we have the freedom to speak without Big Brother's permission. Our freedom to reap the rewards of our capitalist system has raised the standard of living around the world. The profit motive is the engine of that system, and is honorable. But those who cultivate moral confusion for profit should understand this: we will name their names and shame them as they deserve to be shamed. We will contest them for the heart and soul of every child, in every neighborhood. For we who are outraged also have the freedom to speak. If we refuse to condemn evil it is not tolerance but surrender. And we will never surrender.

Let me be specific. One of the companies on the leading edge of coarseness and violence is Time Warner. It is a symbol of how much we have lost. In the 1930s its corporate predecessor, Warner Brothers, made a series of movies, including "G-Men," for the purpose of restoring "dignity and public confidence in the police." It made movies to help the war effort in the early 1940s. Its company slogan, put on a billboard across from the studio, was "Combining Good Citizenship with Good Picture Making."

Today Time Warner owns a company called Interscope Records which columnist John Leo called the "cultural equivalent of owning half the world's mustard gas factories." Ice-T of "Cop Killer" fame is one of Time Warner's "stars." I cannot bring myself to repeat the lyrics of some of the "music" Time Warner promotes. But our children do. There is a difference between the description of evil through art, and the marketing of evil through commerce. I would like to ask the executives of Time Warner a question: Is this what you intended to accomplish with your careers? Must you debase our nation and threaten our children for the sake of corporate profits?

And please don't answer that you are simply responding to the market. Because that is not true. In the movie business, as Michael Medved points out, the most profitable films are the ones most friendly to the family. Last year, the top five grossing films were the blockbusters "The Lion King," "Forrest Gump," "True Lies," "The Santa Clause" and "The Flintstones." To put it in perspective, it has been reported that "The Lion King" made six times as much money as "Natural Born Killers."

The corporate executives who dismiss my criticism should not misunderstand. Mine is not the objection of some tiny group of zealots or an ideological fringe. From inner city mothers to suburban mothers to family in rural America—parents are afraid, and growing angry. There once was a time when parents felt the community of adults was on their side. Now they feel surrounded by forces assaulting their children and their code of values.

This is not a partisan matter. I am a conservative Republican, but I am joined in this fight by moderates, independents, and liberal Democrats. Senator Bill Bradley has spoken eloquently on this subject, as has Senator Paul Simon, who talks of our nation's "crisis of glamorized violence." And leaders of the entertainment industry are beginning to speak up, as well.

Mark Canton, the president of Universal Pictures, said "Any smart business person can see what we must do— make more 'PG'—rated films." He said, "Together . . . we can make the needed changes. If we don't, this decade will be noted in the history books as the embarrassing legacy of what began as a great art form. We will be labeled, 'the decline of an empire.'"

Change is possible—in Hollywood, and across the entertainment industry. There are few national priorities more urgent. I know that good and caring people work in this industry. If they are deaf to the concerns I have raised tonight, it must be because they do not fully understand what is at stake. But we must make them understand. We must make it clear that tolerance does not mean neutrality between love and cruelty, between peace and violence, between right and wrong. Ours is not a crusade for censorship, it is a call for good citizenship.

When I announced I was running for President, I said my mission is to rein in our government, to reconnect the powerful with the values which have made America strong and to reassert America's place as a great nation in the world. Tonight I am speaking beyond this room to some of the most powerful arbiters of our values. Tonight my challenge to the entertainment industry i[s] to accept a calling above and beyond the bottom line—to fulfill a duty to the society which provides its profits. Help our nation maintain the innocence of its children. Prove to us that courage and conscience are alive and well in Hollywood.

Thank you for listening to me tonight. I am grateful for the support you have shown by being here, and feel a great sense of hope and confidence that together we will succeed—not only in this Presidential race, but in our larger mission to reaffirm the goodness and greatness of the United States of America.

Thank you very much.

INFORMATION UNBOUND[3]
ROBERT E. ALLEN

Chair and CEO, AT&T; born Missouri, 1935; grew up in Indiana; B.S., Wabash College, 1957; Harvard University Business School's Program for Management Development, 1965; Vice President with Indiana Bell, Bell of Pennsylvania, and AT&T.

Editors' introduction: Mr. Robert E. Allen, CEO of AT&T, "leads an enterprise that is expanding beyond traditional telecommunications into global information technology and services. By 1997, AT&T will be restructured into three separate, publicly

[3]Delivered at the Carnegie Building, Pennsylvania State University, PA, on October 19, 1995, at 4 p.m.

held companies, each focused on different segments of the information industry: communications services, communications systems and technology, and computers. The communications services company will become the new AT&T, and Mr. Allen will serve as its Chair and CEO." Allen gave the annual James R. and Barbara R. Palmer Chair Lecture in Telecommunications at Pennsylvania State University, entitled "Information Unbound: Its Riches, Risks, and Responsibilities," on October 19, 1995. Allen discussed "the good and bad sides of the information revolution. . . . It was Allen's first major speech since the recent announcement that American Telephone & Telegraph Co. (AT&T), would break into three separate companies to better compete in the industry." Using a teleprompter, Allen spoke in the Carnegie Cinema, housed on the first floor of the Carnegie Building. Attending were students and faculty in communications, business, and engineering. The speech was carried by television to educators, students, and communications professionals at sixty additional college sites. Following the formal presentation, Allen received questions from callers across the U.S. In response to a caller from Arizona concerning whether the poor would have access to the new information technology, Allen answered: "We certainly cannot in any way find ourselves in a position . . . where we have this wonderful technology and haves and have-nots. The government has some role in making sure that doesn't happen, probably more at the state and local level" (David DeKok, Harrisburg *Evening News*, Oct. 20, 1995). Allen apprised the editors of this volume that his purpose was to "explore the coming of the information age—its possibilities, but also its risks and responsibilities." He perceived the response to his address to have been very positive. "During this dramatic time," Dean Brooks noted, "Mr. Allen's recent announcement of the corporate restructuring of AT&T, the world's largest telecommunications organization, cuts to the core of the issues facing the national information infrastructure."

Robert E. Allen's speech: Thank you, Dr. Taylor and Dean Brooks. It's a pleasure to join all of you today. I think, though, that we should settle something right off the bat.

We all know there are certain subjects that are best left unsaid. Those, of course, are also the ones that invariably spring to mind first.

After all, I do own a television. And it's often tuned to sports coverage on the weekend.

The first tie I reached for this morning was blue and white.

And on my way here this morning, warmed by the sight of AT&T's sign on your new home for basketball, I couldn't help but notice Beaver Stadium.

So here's my deal: I won't mention the Nittany Lions football season—if you won't mention that *Fortune* magazine recently described me as "dull as flannel."

So as not to live up to that reputation, I wanted to talk with you today about the future that information is fashioning. It's anything but flannel.

But it's not certain either. No one really knows the exact contours of the age ahead. Even so, it's being compared to the coming of fire, the atom and the Industrial Revolution. It's nothing if not profound.

And, like the students among us, it's just now coming of age. I envy you your times—and the freedoms they promise. But I would also remind you that, just as hellos imply farewells, rights assume certain risks and responsibilities. And your generation, more than most, will confront them as you embark on the digital frontier.

I'd like to explore some of those challenges today. But first I thought I'd paint today's landscape from the perspective of my business.

AT&T used to be defined by the telephone, an everyday "voice-thrower" once described as the shining plastic cousin of a shoe. For all its familiarity, it's now taking on the attributes of both the television and computer. And the convergence of technologies allowing that is promising to transform the way we live, work and play.

The digital revolution is already more reality than vision. And it's moving fast. When this decade began, the Internet was still the province of science and government. The U.S. vice president made news for his spelling, not his support of the Information Superhighway. And an ATM was where you got cash for the weekend.

Today it's estimated that between 30 and 50 million people access the Internet—an ad hoc network that has come to symbolize the freewheeling, sometimes seditious and always interactive nature of things to come.

Meanwhile, the Information Superhighway, still trying to live down its name, is nonetheless speeding up its traffic. It ranges from multimedia networking and electronic commerce to lectures such as this, which can now reach 50 campuses instead of one.

And new technologies, keeping to their brazen pace, may yet have us answering the television and watching the phone.

As the *Financial Times* recently reported, we're moving from POTS—or plain old telephone service—to "pretty awesome new stuff"—also known as PANS.

But the shift from POTS to PANS isn't just a technological shell game. Its reach is pervasive and spreading. It has already rendered national borders obsolete. Now it's erasing the lines delineating entire industries, technologies, products and markets.

In the U.S. alone, for example, at least seven distinct industries, from telecommunications and publishing to personal computing and broadcasting, are merging to create the market known as interactive multimedia.

In some quarters, that is giving rise to once-unlikely mergers—from Disney and ABC/Capital Cities to Time-Warner's link with Turner Broadcasting.

At AT&T, it led to the decision to split ourselves in three.

On September 20, we announced plans to separate AT&T into three publicly traded, global companies focused on communications services, communications systems, and transaction-intensive computing.

Within hours of the announcement financial markets had added $10 billion to the value of the corporation. But the restructuring is not about short-term shareowner value, size or the need to change willy-nilly.

It's about our long-term ability to focus on customers, simplify the business, and take advantage of the growth opportunities in a $1.5 trillion industry that's expected to double in size within 10 years.

With restructuring, each business can become the best and most aggressive global competitor in the world. Each can move even faster to seize opportunities for growth. Each can make decisions and shift direction without having to consider the conflicting strategies of other units.

Some saw in our announcement a reaction to the communications legislation now pending in Congress. Public policy was obviously *a* factor in our decision, but not *the* controlling one. If anything, we're now ahead of the rules we play by.

After all, vertical integration is a snug fit with monopoly power. For us, it had become outdated. With restructuring, we're outfitting ourselves for open competition. And we'd like to see legislation and world markets follow suit.

In the U.S., The Communications Reform Bill is about to go before a joint House and Senate conference committee. But the public in this policy isn't being well served.

As the bill now stands, it would let the Regional Bell Operating Companies compete in long distance even as they maintain a monopoly stranglehold on local service.

In recent weeks, though, we've been encouraged by discussions in Washington. Key members of the House and Senate have said they recognize the bill is unbalanced and they want it corrected before it becomes law. Likewise, the Clinton Administration has warned of a veto if the bill doesn't allow real competition.

Today the U.S. is the world leader in the information industry. In large part, we're first in the market because we were the first of any nation to introduce competition in three parts of the telecommunications industry: long distance, equipment sales, and manufacturing.

But competition's job isn't quite done. It needs to flourish in the local market, as well.

That will mean removing existing barriers that block entry to new competitors in local markets. And it will mean ensuring that real opportunities for competition in local markets exist in practice as well as theory.

I think there's a strong possibility we'll see balanced legislation that all parties can live with. After all the move toward open competition and access in this country, while sometimes plodding, has also been steady.

Two more steps in that direction were taken just last week. In one the FCC lifted AT&T's classification as a "dominant carrier." As such, we'd been required to wait up to 45 days to introduce a new service or change prices. Now we only have to give one day's notice, just like our competitors.

In another move, the Department of Justice proposed to a federal court that U.S. West be allowed to provide both local and long distance service outside of its 14-state territory. The proposal, which affirms a customer's right to choose a long distance carrier, has our backing. We see it as a valuable experiment in introducing real competition and customer choice in the local market.

Elsewhere in the world, competition in telecommunications service is still a novelty. Aside from the U.S. and a handful of other nations, telecommunications in most parts of the world are still provided by state-owned or controlled companies. Yet companies protected as monopolies at home are eager to compete in the open U.S. market.

Competition in many of those nations is endorsed, but not practiced. To prod them to action, there's a growing move to ensure that nations competing in the U.S. provide comparable market access on their home turf. Customers demand it—for they are being denied the benefits of global competition in a world grown economically interdependent.

Indeed, the vision of a global village is close to reality. Work now follows the sun, as time zones replace some clocks. Financial markets electronically move some $3 trillion a day, crossing borders as they please. And information technology is opening global business to all comers, not just the largest firms or most advanced nations.

Being wired in today's world is becoming an economic necessity. Just a one percent increase in teledensity—the number of phone lines relative to population size—raises a nation's GDP by three percent.

Acknowledging the critical role of information technology, the nations of the world are investing more than $1 trillion a week in communications networks. In fact, more will be spent on telecommunications equipment during this decade than in the 119 years since the invention of the telephone.

Today, for example, only three percent of China's 1.2 billion people have phones—a technolological deficit inconsistent with China's hopes of becoming a world economic leader. To correct the imbalance, China adopted a two-pronged approach. It's increasing phone capacity exponentially and leapfrogging over previous generations of technology to land squarely on the information superhighway.

To build the superhighway, China will add 13 million phone lines—the equivalent of a Bell Atlantic—every year until 2000.

By then, their network will be as large as ours in the U.S. And then they plan to pick up [the] pace by 50 percent.

Consider, if you will, the implications in the financial market alone. The information superhighway, coupled with current efforts to reform banking, could speed the day when China's cash society could skip over the checkbook era and leap directly to a cashless age of electronic fund transfers, credit cards and smart cards. There are not a few bankers in other so-called advanced nations who would envy China's position.

Leapfrogging, of course, isnt limited to China. *Business Week* recently reported that the world's most sophisticated networks are in Djibouti, Rwanda, the Maldives and the Solomon Islands. All of their main lines are digital, compared with only half in the U.S.

Meanwhile, Argentina is bringing cellular service to areas that never had any kind of phone service before. And Chile plans to inaugurate a wireless personal communications service network in December—months ahead of the U.S.

For all the potential, though, we shouldn't overlook the fact that half the world's population has yet to make a phone call. There are still many nations where people wait six or seven years for a phone line. And even the exponential growth of global access to the Internet can't erase the fact that one third of the world's people can't read.

And that brings us back to the responsibilities and risk of the digital revolution that I mentioned earlier. For despite its dazzle, technology doesn't come without its downsides. And I'd like to leave you today with a few thoughts on the obligations implied in technological advances enjoyed.

I am often asked, in settings such as this, how higher learning can best prepare students for the changing demands of business.

But truth be told what business wants today is what we wanted yesterday: the student with the mind engaged, the soul inspired. Students schooled, not only in the rigors of a specialty, but also in the social, ethical and political implications of what they do. To expect less in these times is to risk much more.

The Progress & Freedom Foundation, for instance, just released *A Magna Carta for the Knowledge Age*. It asked, in part, who will shape the new civilization rapidly rising to replace industrial society? "Who, in other words, will shape the nature of cyberspace and its impact on our lives and institutions?"

The answer is in this room and among the students joining us at other college settings. For it is your generation, more than mine, that will be defining what it means to be human in a[n] age of packaged reality. And I would hope that definition isn't confined to one discipline or bent of mind.

The challenges of this age, much like its opportunities, are enormous. As the new Magna Carta states: "As humankind explores this new electronic frontier of knowledge, it must confront again the most profound questions of how to organize itself for the common good.

The meaning of freedom, structures of self-government, definition of property, nature of competition, conditions for cooperation, sense of community, and nature of progress will each be redefined for the Knowledge Age—just as they were redefined for a new age of industry some 250 years ago."

And the Progress and Freedom Foundation is optimistic about the potential of the digital revolution. Other voices are not. And you'll need to listen to them also.

You'll need to listen to Mark Slouka, a University of California lecturer who, while not a Luddite, has his concerns. In his book *War of the Worlds*, he says his concerns are based on well-worn truths: "that the free market can unleash forces difficult to control; "that technological innovation has its own logic, often separate from questions of values and ethics; and that some technologies—particularly those that promise (or threaten) to transform human culture as we know it—bear watching."

Slouka would have you question whether virtual reality leads us to accept the copy for the original. Will we forget, he asks, that "virtually dead means alive; that something virtually true or virtually real is false"? And will we, in the end, mistake mass opinion for our own?

This isn't simple stuff. And as technology advances, the questions are bound to get harder.

In the latest edition of *Wired* magazine, John Perry Barlow poses a question that may simplify things. "When we behold some new species of technology," he says, "we should ask ourselves one question: does it connect or does it separate?"

Barlow argues that the telephone, more often than not, connects; while the TV is predisposed to separate. And the technologies of the digital revolution? He wants them to serve his purpose: "Which is to connect. To make contact. To wake up, shocked by the voltage of increased interaction between properties of humanity in my heart and those in yours. To be whole."

In the end, perhaps that is your biggest challenge: to ground technology in what it is that makes us human. To take what technology will give us and turn it to the common good.

I would urge you to do that. But I would also like to leave you with a caution in that regard. I would ask you not to confuse information with knowledge or wisdom. I would ask you not to turn libraries into simple warehouses for facts. I would, in short, ask you to consider information, not as an end in itself, but as raw material that can be magically transformed by human imagination.

The dictionary, whether it's *Webster's* or a Web site's, is a marvelous compendium of facts, for instance. On page 139 of my collegiate edition, I can locate the term "beauty" among its companions: bebop, beckon, and becloud.

"Beauty" is defined in a quite sufficient, worky kind of way. It suits my needs—but not my soul.

For that I have to turn to someone like John Keats who, on examining a Grecian urn wrought by the high technology of its day, found humanity itself. Keats concluded, "Beauty is truth, truth beauty,—that is all ye know on earth, and all ye need to know."

Put another way, on the road with information, I would hope your destination is still the intersection where knowlege and wisdom meet truth and beauty.

Thank you for the opportunity to share my views. I'd be happy now to take your questions.

VII. RELIGION

THE VALUE OF HOSPITALITY[1]
Alexander M. Schindler

Rabbi; President, Union American Hebrew Congregations, New York City; born Munich, Germany, 1925; B.A., City College of New York, 1950; M.H.L., Hebrew Union College, 1952; editor; Bronze Star; Purple Heart; Solomon Bublick Prize.

Editors' introduction: Rabbi Alexander M. Schindler addressed the First Convocation on Jewish/Muslim Relations in America on March 26, 1995. Schindler told the editors of this volume that "our desire to meet with representatives of the American Muslim community was impelled by the hope that such a dialogue—feasible as it is here in America, with its devotion to the principle of pluralism—would enable us to move toward the attainment of our shared purpose: the peaceful coexistence of Arabs and Jews in the Middle East, and the drawing nearer even in this land of the two faith-communities that are truly bound to one another by a common history and destiny." Larry Hartstein (*Chicago Tribune*, March 27, 1995) noted that 250 Muslim and Jewish leaders from around the country met at this convocation, mainly persons "representing Judaism's Reform movement and African-American Muslims." There were leaders of the Jewish and American Islamic communities, Jewish and Muslim academics, and lay people. For security reasons, the meeting was not widely publicized. Rabbi Gary M. Bretton-Granatoor said he hoped the conference would "spur interfaith dialogues across the country." Dr. Mohammed Cheema, President of the American Muslim Council, indicated that the mission of the session was "to create a relationship, friendship, understanding, and cooperation." Jan M. Brahms observed that, while the convocation "began with diplomatic niceties, more significant were the opportunities for serious discussion where genuine differences and problems were not ignored" (*Capital Times*, April 1, 1995).

[1]Delivered at the Northshore Congregation Israel, Glencoe, IL, on March 26, 1995, at 11 a.m.

Schindler spoke to 250 persons gathered at Northshore Congregation Israel in Glencoe, Illinois. In his address, he emphasized the value of hospitality, the importance of dialogue, and the two religion's common struggle against a materialistic culture. According to the *Chicago Tribune*, Warith Deen Mohammed, Leader of the American Muslim Community, who also spoke, described Islam as a religion of peace, "expressed empathy with Jewish suffering under the Nazi regime," but indicated that Israel had done "some ugly things" since the country was established in 1948. Mohammad, who embraced Schindler twice, counseled that "We are to have compassion, and we are to be on the side of the suffering people always." After Schindler and Mohammad's opening remarks, the rabbis, imams, and academics in attendance met in small workshops on such topics as the impact of Middle East peace on Jewish-Muslim relations, biblical and koranic images of Abraham, and community-based joint action.

Alexander M. Schindler's speech: It is a privilege which I greatly appreciate to be here and to help initiate this Jewish/Muslim Convocation, and to share this platform with the Imam Mohammed, the universally recognized spiritual leader of America's Moslem community.

There is a verse in the Torah that inspires me in relation to this remarkable gathering. It is in the Book of Genesis which tells us that when our father *Hazrat*, our father Abraham, breathed his last, his sons Isaac and Ishmael "buried him in the Cave of Machpelah . . . "

Isaac and Ishmael, mourning together at their father's tomb. . . . Is it not ever thus, a common tragedy that draws erstwhile foes together . . .

Isaac and Ishmael, mourning together over their father's tomb. Elsewhere in Scripture we encounter these brothers in opposition to one another—as antagonists, as sibling rivals, yet at the same time as co-victims of their father's complex psyche. Ishmael, especially, is subject in the Jewish tradition to a diminution of his character. Centuries before the founding of Islam, rabbinic literature sought to deflect the blame for his expulsion from Abraham and Sarah to Ishmael and Hagar themselves. Ishmael is described as an "idolater," or as an avaricious son "craving to inherit his father's entire estate." Yet here, the Torah itself reports, in its typically spare manner, a reconciliation between the brothers. Here the Torah itself reminds us in its great wisdom, of their *shared paternity*, and of the values that *both* men inherited.

It is those values that bring us together, and which we embody in our coming together this day: first and foremost, the value of hospitality. The tent of our father Abraham, so the Jewish tradition tells us, was open on all four sides, so that all the weary and hungry sojourners would feel free to enter. "This teaches us," so say the rabbis of the Talmud, "that the practice of hospitality, the welcoming of strangers, is more important even than is the welcoming of God." Indeed, both to the Jew and to the Muslim, hospitality is very much the equivalent of "inviting God into one's home," for we never know when our visitors will prove to be not ordinary nomads but angel messengers.

Scripture also shows us that the *site* of hospitality, the place of encounter is crucial to the outcome, for in different places we are different beings, different in our measure of power; different in our measure of security. Thus was Abraham our father commanded to leave the safety and familiarity of his home and to journey to a strange land before his vision of the One God and his mission to his fellow human beings would become clear. And thus perhaps, we in America, as Muslim and Jew, are better able to reclaim our common heritage and to engage in fruitful dialogue than we are in our father's house. Aye, it is the great tragedy of contemporary life, is it not, that at the Cave of Machpelah, there in ancient Hebron, Muslim and Jew are still incapable of dialogue, or even of peaceful silence. I therefore pray—and I would ask all of us to pray—that the process of reconciliation that at long last is dawning in the land of our forefathers and foremothers will continue to brighten to a full and high noon.

But here in America, the possibilities of dialogue are spread before us like a midday feast on the table. For here we are both religious minorities, united in our awareness of the democratic grants and freedoms that protect us from the homogenizing desires of a dominant majority. Here the great principle of the separation of church and state secures the sanctity of our religious autonomy. Here we will not become victims of a Crusader's sword or an Inquisitor's rack, not as long as we work together to buttress that protective wall of separation.

We are the heirs of still another patrimony bequeathed to us by Abraham. We are both communities of committed God-seekers, inheritors of traditions whose essential mission is to actualize, in our every endeavor, the redeeming force that we call God.

Here in America, we are engaged not in a debate about one another's truth, but in a common struggle against a materialistic culture that declares truth to be but another commodity, something that can be used, that can be bought, or sold to the highest bidder. Here the struggle against moral relativism, can unite us. The struggle against the worship of the Almighty dollar, against the idolatrous Cult of the Individual, against the *daylily*, as the Koran calls it, the "misguidedness," the "false path" of modern secularism—this is the struggle that can cause us to come together in our activities and in our prayers.

In short, America both facilitates and makes necessary our dialogue. The effectiveness of that dialogue, however, will be due to something more than a receptive environment or a political imperative.

It will be due in the first instance to our willingness to be honest with ourselves, to engage in what the Jewish tradition calls a *cheshban hanefesh*, a self-reckoning of the soul. Every journey to our fellow men and women is first a painful journey inward to our own existence: a confrontation with our own past and present imperfections, a wrestling match with the demons in our own soul.

Second, the effectiveness of our dialogue will depend on our willingness to be honest each within our *own* communities. The wounds inflicted by the fulminations of a Farrakhan or a Meir Kahane cannot be assuaged by caution or polite silence. "Death and life are in the power of the tongue," the Bible instructs us. And the Talmud adds the teaching that "silence is tantamount to confession to an admission of guilt." Jews, alas, do not need Scripture to understand the importance of speaking out against hatred, whatever and wherever its source. It is a knowledge that centuries of persecution have engraved on our hearts.

Third, and finally, the effectiveness of our dialogue will depend on our willingness to be honest with one another, on the resolve not to feed each other pablum, not to say only what we think will please the other to hear, but always to tell the truth as we perceive it, to assert our convictions with passion even as we remain respectful of our disagreements.

I would enter into this dialogue, therefore, by confessing to a feeling of vulnerability.

Mine is a feeling so typically Jewish, and yet it would probably appear to be to many American Muslims as a neurosis at best, or a deception at worst. Nevertheless, the truth is that I experience myself on this podium not as president of a multi-million member religious community, but as an aging member of a tiny, tiny people—only 18 million strong throughout the world and barely one generation recovered from a genocide that wiped one out of every three Jewish men, women and children. I stand here less as a secure citizen of our powerful United States, and more as a German Jewish refugee from Hitlerism, a Jewish survivor on the banks of that long river of European anti-Semitism. I stand here less as a liberal, peace oriented ally of a militarily strong Israel, and more as a desperately concerned lover of Zion whose devotion to Israel can barely be contained within that tiny nation's ever-threatened borders.

To be sure, now, there is a difference between perception and reality. I fully recognize the difference between my feelings of personal vulnerability as a Jew and my knowledge of that actual if tenuous historical empowerment that Jews have experienced in both Israel and America during the past four decades. No longer are we the meek of the earth, as we were for millennia. We have gained a degree of temporal power, enough, we pray, to prevent our "meekness" from ever again leading to victimization; power, as well, to test the conscience of the Jewish people and to test our mettle as peacemakers.

Still, as a Jew, I approach you with that sense of personal and communal vulnerability. I am in awe of your numbers and your resurgence as a force in the world—one billion followers of the Islamic faith worldwide. I am overawed by your geographic scope and resources, and by your racial, national, and ethnic diversity.

On the other hand, as an American who is steeped in the consciousness of multiculturalism, and alert to all signs of prejudice, I am aware of how you, as American Muslims, might indeed experience your own particular sense of vulnerability. For all of your growing numbers worldwide, you are only 4 1/2 million strong across this continent—and with fewer mosques throughout this nation than are sometimes Christian churches in a single city! And notwithstanding your religious unity, your diversity of ethnic and national-origin serves as a counterweight to your becoming the kind of a political "block" that has, for example, made the highly organized evangelic Christian movement so effective and powerful. The Arab-American majority among you suffers exceedingly from stereotyping . . . from ascribing to all the guilt of some . . . from associating all Arab-Americans with loathsome Islamic fundamentalist terrorism. Your media image is one of parody and xenophobia. Your "foreignness" is causally assumed regardless of the extent of your assimilation. Never mind that a vital Muslim presence is as longstanding in America as that of Jews or Catholics. Never mind whether you are an American Moslem with roots in Africa or in Asia or in the Middle East, in Iran or in Eastern Europe, yet one hears only of the Judeo-Christian tradition, but one never hears of a "Judeo-Christian-Islamic" continuum.

As for the African American among you, your vulnerability in America is an existential state. Racist oppression knows no boundaries either at your cradle or grave, or at the threshold of your home, or even at the portals of your soul. You are an endangered species in America, a caged and mistreated species, and you have been so for nearly four centuries, nearly as long as the Bible tells us that the Hebrew people were enslaved in Egypt. We know full well, moreover, that the contemporary Pharaohs' new contract with America is first and foremost a contract on you and on you[r] children.

These are the flashes of pain that I glimpse, my friends, when I look into your eyes. These are the flashes of fear that I ask you to recognize when you look into mine. From that glance, from that recognition of our complex fluid identities—identities of pride and fear, of empowerment and vulnerability—our dialogue can proceed. It can proceed in a uniquely American voice, for it is here, in this multicultural stew, that fanaticism cannot, must not harden. It is here that Ishmael and Isaac can look into each other's eyes, and see the essential bond of humanness and brotherhood that exceeds all differences.

It is here, too, that our prayers can resonate in a healing harmony—a harmony that might quell some of the discordance that marks our troubled times. For the truth is that, for all our multicultural "difference" in America, spiritual malaise and emptiness is our common lot. We see it manifest in the violence that erupts in every corner, daily. We see it manifest in the angry politics that brings the spirit of meanness and scapegoating to Washington D.C. rather than a sense of compassion and justice. We see that malaise and emptiness in the statistics of vast wealth and widespread poverty that are the shame of our nation—statistics that testify to dehumanization and isolation, to a society that has spurned its sense of social responsibility, that has lost its ability to respond.

There is a great hunger that has seized our age, my friends, a hunger for values, a hunger for community, a hunger for pathways to a higher consciousness, a hunger to serve something and someone besides the fragmented Self. The prophet, Amos, spoke of such a hunger when he said: "Behold the day cometh, sayeth the Lord God, that I will set a famine in the land, not a famine of bread nor a thirst for water, but of hearing the words of the Lord."

This is the hunger that we begin to satisfy by breaking bread together this day.

Perhaps it is more than coincidence that yesterday's Torah portion *Shemini* enunciates the laws of *kashrut*, the laws of what we may and may not eat, that also forms a part of the shared values and shared perceptions of our respective tradition. May it be God's will that the morsels of religious dialogue that we are sharing today be multiplied miraculously until the Great Hunger that has seized our age will be transmuted into a Feast of Thanksgiving throughout America and throughout the world.

A BETTER COUNTRY[2]
RANDALL L. SAXON

Senior Pastor, First Presbyterian Church, Peoria, IL; born Waverly, NY, 1947; B.A., Mansfield University, 1969; M. Div., Princeton Theological Seminary, 1973; D. Min., Drew University, 1992; senior pastor in PA, TX, and NY; adjunct faculty member; author.

Editors' introduction: On Sunday, November 19, 1995, in preparation for Thanksgiving, Dr. Randall Lee Saxon addressed the congregation and guests at the First Presbyterian Church in Peoria, Illinois. Saxon delivered his sermon to a total audience of

[2]Delivered at Peoria First Presbyterian Church, IL, on November 19, 1995, at 8:30 a.m. and 11:00 a.m.

three-hundred. Attending were persons of all ages from the seventeen communities the church serves as well as students from Bradley University and Illinois Central College. At each service the sermon was preceded by singing and prayers for the community, the nation, and the legislative, executive, and judicial branches of government, and for the work of the United Nations around the world. Saxon explained to the editors of this volume that the purposes of his talk were to recall the journey of the Pilgrims and their effort to found a better country; to explain how an exemplary faith would be required to meet contemporary cultural issues; and to encourage his parishioners to become more active in the world—to adopt specific roles by which they could serve the common good and address local, national, and global needs. Saxon said he received "a great number of enthusiastic responses . . . affirming the concept that cultural change begins when interested individuals commit time, energy, and personal talents to speak to real need; college students were particularly receptive to the call for action, as were local business leaders." When Ray LaHood, member of the House of Representatives from Illinois, inserted Saxon's sermon in the *Congressional Record* (Dec. 5, 1995), he added: "At a time when Congress—and the country—is wrestling with devolution of a Federal Government and personal responsibility, Dr. Saxon's words leapt from the pages as I read them."

Randall L. Saxon's speech: By faith Abraham obeyed when he was called to set out for a place that he was to receive as an inheritance; and he set out, not knowing where he was going . . .

Therefore from one person, and this one as good as dead, descendants were born, "as many as the stars of heaven and as the innumerable grains of sand by the seashore."

All of these died in faith without having received the promises, but from a distance they saw and greeted them. They confessed that they were strangers and foreigners on the earth, for people who speak in this way make it clear that they are seeking a homeland.

If they had been thinking of the land that they had left behind, they would have had opportunity to return. But as it is, they desire a better country, that is, a heavenly one. Therefore God is not ashamed to be called their God; indeed, he has prepared a city for them . . .

Christians are always in search of a better country. Those who take their faith seriously endeavor to move beyond a feel-good religion to a follow-Jesus faith. Such a faith demands that we continue on our journey of discovery, to build upon the good that was present before us, to bring down the walls that divide us, to bridge chasms—real or imagined—that separate us. Christians are always in search of a better country.

As with the people of the early Christian Church and as with the people who followed the patriarchs of early Judaism, the way of the Christian is the way of the Pilgrim.

Those who have the good fortune to visit the Old Town of Rotterdam, in the Netherlands, may visit still the Pilgrim Fathers' Church—as it is yet called—in which the Scrooby Pilgrims and the Leyden Pilgrims held their last service prior to entering on their incredible journey to discover a better country. Those staunch and visionary forebears of ours worshipped together, then made their way down to the water where they boarded the *Speedwell* to begin their westward journey. Written bold upon a plaque secured to a warehouse on that Rotterdam waterfront is a commemoration to the departure of the Pilgrims.

From The Netherlands, the little ship bearing the Pilgrim band sailed to Plymouth, England. In the English port, after a period of time, the Pilgrims boarded a larger ship, the *Mayflower*, and set sail for the brave new world awaiting them across the dark and brooding Atlantic waters. As in Rotterdam, so in Plymouth one may today read of this bold departure of the Pilgrims, commemorating in words writ upon the grand Mayflower Monument the extraordinary event of the journey to discover a better country and thus a better life.

We can imagine that these pious people reflected on the words of Hebrews 11 in the Holy Scripture: "People who speak in this way make it clear that they are seeking a homeland. If they had been thinking of the land that they had left behind, they would have had opportunity to return. But, as it is, they desired a better country. . . . "

We know that many factors figured in the Pilgrims' decision to leave home and cross the great sea in search of a new land, a better country. As children in public and private schools across America, we are given opportunity to re-examine the religious and political persecutions and deep yearning of the human spirit which emboldened the Pilgrims to set sail for America. They sought an opportunity to worship as they thought fitting, to engage themselves in self-determination and the utilization of individual gifts for the common purpose of building community. They yearned for a government which would be best described by an American president 243 years after they sailed from Plymouth, a government in which the common people were *involved*; a government of the people, for the people, and by the people.

Yet, strange-seeming upon first consideration, these same Pilgrims who were willing to leave hearth and homeland for a wild and distant country viewed themselves *as strangers and foreigners on the earth*. As people of God, they sought with great diligence to live as people of faith in an often faithless world. These Pilgrims held values which transcended the simple "be a good person, be nice to your neighbor" values in human relationships. These values demanded much more of the individual and of society than simply "being nice"; these values demanded one's life commitment to the upbuilding of the kingdom of God. It is no wonder historians who trace the Euro-American pilgrimage from its inception to the present day call the experiment of the Pilgrims by the name "Zion in the Wilderness." There was purpose and commitment in what the Pilgrims set out to accomplish. Their journey was to a *better country*!

The Church today is called to remember it is still on that same journey that set sail the Pilgrims so long ago. "The Church exists today as resident aliens, an adventurous colony in a society of unbelief. As a society of unbelief, Western culture is devoid of a sense of journey, of adventure, because it lacks belief in much more than the cultivation of an ever-shrinking horizon of self-preservation and self-expression." [*Resident Aliens* by Hauerwas, S. and Willimon, W. H.]

The ancient Hebrew patriarchs, the disciples of Jesus of Nazareth, the Pilgrims of the seventeenth century, the visionaries who held "these Truths to be self-evident, that all Men are created equal, that they are endowed by their Creator with certain unalienable Rights, that among these are Life, Liberty, and the Pursuit of Happiness," the founders of this visionary congregation—First Presbyterian Church of Peoria, IL—160 years ago, all were traveling the road to a better country. They had, as the Rev. Dr. Martin Luther King has said, "a dream."

To tell the truth, that dream, those visions, have taken on the fearful characteristics of a nightmare. The nation—the *better*

country—the Pilgrim people sought to discover and build upon
has drifted loose from it moral moorings into a sea of self-
centeredness, a Devil's Triangle of you-do-your-thing-and-I'll-
do-mine-and-that's-all-that-matters-anyway   boorishness   that
shakes the very foundation of our society.

The home of the brave and land of the free in the 1990s—
fifteen generations after the Pilgrims landed on the Massachus-
setts shore—has become the home of the fearful and the land of
the imprisoned. America today has more citizens in prison, per
capita, than any other nation in the free world. The experience
of being "free" is what many do *not* experience.

We have winked at the discord in our nation. We have turned
away from taking personal responsibility to become change
agents involved in the creation of a better country. We have come
to blame the three branches of our federal government for our
troubles, making scapegoats of the very people we have elected
to lead us. It is hard to hear and harder again to admit, but many
of us do not experience freedom as the Pilgrims sought to create
it. We are fearful instead. Our everyday lives point to this truth.
Consider: " . . . our overstocked medicine cabinets, burglar
alarms, vast ghettos, and drug culture. Eighteen-hundred New
Yorkers are murdered every year by their fellow citizens in a city
whose police department is larger than the standing army of
many nations!" [*Resident Aliens*]

We have become fearful of one another. We seem to have lost
our way on that journey to a better country. Where is the vision
of the Pilgrim people? Why do we cower in fear and confusion,
choosing to attempt to outrun the darkness rather than turn and
say with conviction, "Enough!" Those people of varied races and
religious traditions and ages who have taken such a stand against
corruption in their individual communities have made a difference, they have shined a light into the darkness and recaptured
a vision of a better country. May God bless them, and our native
land!

The time has come again for the people of God to become a
Pilgrim people! The time has come again for the people of God
to say what they believe, and to set sail on a journey that will lead
us all to a better country. What am I saying? Leave America for
another place?

Not at all! Despite her flaws, America is yet the greatest nation
on earth, for people still risk their lives to make this land their

home. Hear me now! I am calling us to recapture the vision of a better country. And to lift up that vision. I am calling us to work together, beginning right here in our own community, to shape a better country so that the little children around us can grow up in a better world. I am calling us to be done with the idiocy of self-centered pettiness that only desecrates, divides, and denigrates the Word of God. I am calling us to catch the vision of a *better country*, and to lift it high in the name of our blessed Lord, Jesus Christ, who has already journeyed ahead of us, calling: "Follow me!"

How do we do this? How do we answer this call? We begin by doing away with the habit of blaming others for our troubles. We become more proactive and less reactive. I say this to you in response to the challenge before us:

1. Pray without ceasing that God will use you and this congregation to build a better country. Every great change in the nation began in the minds and hearts and spirits of the people who helped make this country great. Change may be facilitated "out there," but it must begin in here, in the mind and heart and spirit of the individual. And in the the home towns of America.

2. Pray to forgive those who divide and deride; counsel them to repent and turn to the Lord, so their vision may be outward and upward rather than inward and downward. Remember John Kennedy's words: "Ask not what your country can do for you, ask what you can do for your country!" Then do it.

3. Open your eyes and your mind to see where your unique, personal gifts can be used to help make life better. For example, offer to ring a bell at a Salvation Army kettle, join hands with others at work in one of our city soup kitchens or other missions, assist as a hospital volunteer, give blood: one pint of that vital fluid may save a life, sign on the line on the back of your driver' s license and commit yourself to becoming an organ donor (hundreds of thousands of lives could be saved annually if more of us would do this), visit the hospitalized, run an errand for one who is ill, comfort the afflicted, challenge the comfortable, teach in our Sunday School. You get the idea. The need is great; open your eyes and minds and respond.

4. Contact our elected representatives and urge them to remember and act on the words of our sixteenth president, that our govermnent may be of, by and for *the people*. Rather than deride the people you elected to represent you, work with them to shape a brighter, better future for all who call America home.

5. Live each day as if it were your last, devoting energy to those profoundly simple acts of discipleship we discover by lifting up faith, hope, and love. And, in that instant, make a difference for good and to God's glory in the life of someone else. Do you begin to realize what a radical difference you can initiate simply by lifting up the values and mores which helped build this country, those aspects of national character which begin on our hearths and in our hearts as we teach our children about God and goodness and grace?

Yes, Christians are always in search of a better country. Those who take their faith seriously endeavor to move beyond a feel-good religion to a follow-Jesus faith. The choice, really, is up to you. You can sit morosely by, captured by a culture of complaint and compliance, or you can let the living God fill your sails with the wind of His Spirit, empowering you to move forward on that journey to a better country.

The America of tomorrow awaits your decision to act. Decide wisely, pilgrim, for you touch the trembling, fragile future with your individual hands and hearts. May God bless America. May God bless you. Amen.

DREAMS: THE ORIGIN OF SUCCESS[3]
COURTNEY L. WATSON

Science and Technology Research Scholar student, Yale University; born Atlanta, GA, 1977; (MS)2 Graduate in Mathematics and Science for Minority Students, Phillips Academy, 1994; Girl Scout Gold and Silver Award, 1994–95; Congressional Medal Winner, 1995; Tandy Technology Most Outstanding Student in Mathematics, Science, and Computer Science, 1995.

Editors' introduction: On June 11, 1995, in her Valedictory speech, Ms. Courtney Leron Watson addressed approximately 5,000 persons attending Benjamin E. Mays High School graduation exercises at the Civic Center in Atlanta, Georgia. Watson de-

[3]Delivered at Benjamin E. Mays High School, Atlanta, GA, on June 11, 1995, at 8:30 p.m.

scribed for the editors the dramatic nature of the ceremony in which she participated: "The audience consisted of Atlanta Public School Board members and the families and friends of the graduates. The speech was preceded by a moment of silence for a lost classmate, the singing of the class song, and the Salutatory Address. As my class and I concluded an excerpt from the song, 'The Impossible Dream,' the house lights were dimmed and my class stood and held lights which formed a star. At this point, I was standing before the microphone." Speaking from memory, she "began . . . by discussing dreams." When she finished the address, the class sang "Hold on to Your Dreams," while dancers wearing lights, performed; then, during a final light show, the class stood to form the letters MH, representing Mays High.

Watson explained to the editors that her purpose was "to encourage the graduating class to dream about the future in relation to ourselves as well as our families, our communities, and our world. My motive was to provoke my classmates to think about the obstacles we must conquer in order to reach our goals." "As a Born-Again Christian," Watson noted, "I was inspired by the teachings of the Holy Bible. From personal experiences, I have seen the teachings of the Bible help me on several occasions. Naturally, I wanted to share my knowledge with my classmates in hopes of conveying ideas which can change their lives for the better." To persuade the audience, Watson "created the image of one's dream being a seed to be sown in the Garden of Life. I used imagery to discuss the positive and negative inhabitants of the Garden of Life which influence the growth and development of one's dreams." Watson was pleased with the audience's reaction. "I received a standing ovation . . . and was encouraged verbally throughout my delivery." The speech was broadcast on local educational television several times. The *Atlanta Journal & Constitution* (June 15, 1955) and the *New York Times* (June 11, 1995) carried excerpts. Watson received many supportive telephone calls and an invitation to air the tape on another local cable television show.

Courtney L. Watson's speech: Dreams are the origin of success; however, do not let your personal desires dominate your dreams. Dream for our families that they will become or continue to be strong and united. Dream for our communities that the beauty of their diversity will be appreciated by their fellow neighbors.

Dream for our world that it will ultimately be a place of the people, by the people, and for the people.

I am a pursuer because I know that reaching the stars depends on one's aspirations. I am an achiever, as I know that it takes dedication, devotion, and diligence to accomplish any task. I am a dreamer because I realize that dreams are the origin of success. To pursue, to achieve, and to dream will demand that we not be deterred by confusion, fear, or doubt. There will be people who will try to discourage us, ridicule us, and laugh at us, but we must continue to hold fast to our dreams despite frustrations.

According to the Word of God in Ephesians Chapter Six, we must keep our feet shod with the preparation of the gospel of peace and victory. We must fight our battles with the sword of the spirit and with determination and tenacity. We must protect ourselves with the shield of faith and with confidence. We must guard our virtue with the breastplate of righteousness and with morality. We must safeguard ourselves with the helmet of salvation. When we put on *this* armor *PRAISE GOD!* we will definitely be ready for the battle.

Our dream is a seed. We must sow it. We must fertilize our dream with perseverance; we must water our dream with patience; we must nurture our dream with faith; and we must expose our dream to the sunshine of prayer whose beauty can illuminate *any* situation.

However, [there] will be trespassers who will enter our garden of dreams to try and destroy the seeds we have sown. Therefore, we must protect our seed from being eaten by the deadly vultures we know as drugs and alcohol. In order to preserve the seed, pluck out the weeds of promiscuity and the thorns of uncleanliness which uproot to strangle the life out of the seed. Shelter the seed from the fangs of the envious snake which carries its destructive venom of jealousy and covetousness. Do not be swayed by these intruders!

My fellow classmates, these are the words of wisdom I leave with you as your class valedictorian. Dream not only for yourselves, but dream for others as well. Nurture your dream as a seed sown in the soil of life. These traits will develop a harvest that will blossom into the fruits of success, the fruits of accomplishment, and the fruits of victory!

In the words of Dr. Benjamin Elijah Mays, "It is within your power to dream, to build air castles, to think great thoughts, to aim at the stars, and to grasp at the moon." My dear classmates, this is our challenge! We must follow the advice of Langston Hughes, the poet laureate of the Harlem Renaissance who urged us to hold fast to our dreams for if dreams die, life is a broken-winged bird that cannot fly. Classmates—hold on to your dream, hold on to your dream, *hold on* to your dream!

VIII. CONTINUING EDUCATION

THE VALUES OF UNIONS[1]
AMY JO BRINDLEY

Graduate of Southeast Polk High School, Runnells, IA, 1996; born 1978; Vice President, French Club; track team; Juvenile Diabetes Foundation; employed part-time, day-care center.

Editors' introduction: On April 6, 1995, Ms. Amy Jo Brindley, then sixteen years old and a junior in high school, spoke from a prepared text to between five and six hundred workers who were striking the Bridgestone/Firestone plant in Des Moines, Iowa. Ms. Brindley's father, Charley, a member of the United Rubber Workers, was one of the strikers; he had worked at the plant for seventeen years. Ms. Brindley's words were included among the "highlights of the rally" broadcast by WOI-TV and KCCI-TV. Senator Tom Harkin of Iowa, in the *Congressional Record*, advised his colleagues to "read the words of this impressive young American." Brindley told the editors of this volume that she "wanted to express to everyone that a strike affects family members and friends of striking union members. To achieve my purpose, I used patriotism, cause and effects, and personal testimony." In the audience were strikers, family members, supportive union members from teamsters, autoworkers, AFSME, electricians, Democratic Party representatives, and religious leaders. In addition to Brindley, several others spoke. In the keynote address, The Reverend Jesse Jackson said he fought for all employees, for "workers are becoming whiter and more middle-class every day. The fundamental issue is not black and white, it's wrong and right" (Jim Pollock, *Des Moines Register*, April 7, 1995).

When her classmates visited Washington, D.C. for their class trip, because of a lack of family funds due to the strike, Brindley remained home and worked. Because he "was so moved by" Brindley's speech, and the fact that she missed her class tour,

[1]Delivered at the United Rubber Workers Rally, Des Moines, IA, on April 6, 1995, at 4:00 p.m.

Jackson sponsored a trip to Washington, D.C. for Ms. Brindley, her sister and mother. In the Capital, she met President Clinton in the oval office during the taping of his weekly radio speech, and with Senator Harkin. On May 21, 1995, the United Rubber Workers called off their strike. If Brindley were to offer advice to teenagers, she would say: "you've got to believe in yourself. Take your opportunity and see what happens" (Margaret Ludington, *Altoona Herald*, May 25, 1995).

Amy Jo Brindley's speech: As a teenage daughter of a United Rubber Worker, who's been on strike for the past 9 months, I'd like to point out that this strike involves many, many people and is just NOT limited to the union members and their employer. Bridgestone/Firestone has invaded the lives of the entire family with their inexcuseable hunger for corporate greed.

I feel that it is important to recognize the numerous family members who have fallen victim to the ruthless demands set forth by Bridgestone/Firestone.

Being a teenager is never easy, but having to deal with the additional stress this labor dispute has brought about, has made it even more challenging. Many friendships have been broken apart throughout this strike. I, myself, have had friendships that have suffered great setbacks because of my pro labor beliefs. I believe that it is the lack of education that a lot of people have concerning the Union. I strongly believe that we need to educate and promote the values and the importance regarding unions. As members of the United Rubber Workers are attempting to hold on to what fellow members have fought to gain in the past years of joining together at the bargaining table. If we don't educate people, what will the future hold, not just for my generation but the following generations also?

I am a junior at Southeast Polk High School. As juniors, we are offered the opportunity to go to Washington D.C. and New York for the United Nations Trip. This trip is only offered to juniors. Because of the strike it was financially impossible for me to go with my fellow classmates. It was very difficult for me to watch my friends, including my best friend, as they prepared for this venture with great anticipation, and again when they returned and shared with me their special memories that I was not a part of. Under different circumstances I would have been among my fellow classmates, but again, due to Brigestone/Firestone's desire for complete control, I was cheated out of a significant, once-in-a-life-time opportunity.

One of Bridgestone/Firestone's most appalling scare tactics that has personally touched myself and my family was the elimination of health care benefits, 90 days into this strike. My sister, Angie, and I are both insulin dependant diabetics. Consequently, it is of utmost importance that we have medical insurance to maintain and control this dreaded disease. It has been impossible for us to find an alternate insurance policy that covers our diabetes. Therefore, my parents have been forced to pay the enormous monthly premiums for the company's Cobra Coverage, adding to the already overwhelming financial burdens families are facing during this work stoppage due to this strike.

I have briefly touched on just a "few" of the intrusions this company has used to manipulate the lives of innocent people. But, on the other hand, some things I don't think this heartless company counted on, is . . . that I've also gained many things. Things that you can't put a material value on. Such as, a new understanding of what the union is truly about, the importance of solidarity, the significance of the support that we've received from fellow unions and citizens. The outpouring of generosity so many different individuals have extended has been astounding. Even though Bridgestone/Firestone has taken away our paycheck and temporarily left us financially strapped; they'll NEVER take away our dignity! Thank you.

BENEFITS AND RESPONSIBILITIES[2]
BRITT ROGERS

Student, Rhodes College, Memphis, TN; born Tupelo, MS, 1976; Salutatorian, Tupelo High School, MS, with 4.0 grade average; National Council of Teachers of English Writing Award; Robert C. Byrd Scholarship; Cambridge College Scholarship; Gum Tree Writing Contest winner.

---

[2]Delivered at the Tupelo Coliseum in Mississippi, on May 24, 1995, at 7:00 p.m.

Editors' introduction: On May 24, 1995, in Mississippi, Brittain ("Britt") Allen Rogers IV presented this salutatory address at the Tupelo High School commencement exercise in the Tupelo Coliseum to an audience of about 2,000. Rogers read the text to the graduating class and their families and friends, an audience of African-Americans and whites. The speech was broadcast on WTUP-1490 local AM radio, and excerpted in the *New York Times* (June 11, 1995). Timeka Jones, a fellow student, introduced Rogers as the speaker. Rogers told the editors of this volume that he wanted to "address the many different backgrounds and interests that the families of the Tupelo Public School system share." To do this "I used local cultural icons to capture my audience's attention, and then supplemented the local aspects of my speech with quotes from Tennyson and others. I also recounted my first day of school and paralleled that challenge to the challenge facing all graduates." His speech was well received.

Britt Rogers' speech: Dr. Mike Walters, Superintendent of Education; Members of the School Board; Administrators at Central Office; Mr. Dale Dobbs, Principal of Tupelo High School; Administrators, Faculty, and Staff of Tupelo High School; Parents, Guests, and fellow classmates of the graduating class of 1995.

Mom awakened me extra early that morning to start preparing for my big day. I carefully stowed my brand new Trapper Keeper, decorated on all sides with baseball stickers, inside my backpack. I checked my supplies: three pencils (meticulously sharpened), one bottle of Elmer's glue, and a pair of the blunt scissors because Mom said I wasn't old enough to use the good kind yet. I put on my best pair of red shorts, my favorite green shirt, and my blue striped socks that came up past my knees. After a breakfast of Froot Loops and milk, Mom marched me down the street to the bus stop. After a few minutes, the pungent odor of carbon monoxide filled the air as the bus pulled to a stop and opened its doors. With a tearful good-bye, my mother waved at me as I rambled off toward my first day of school. I can still remember arriving at Church Street Elementary School, staring wide-eyed at the enormous building, and wondering how many wonderful mysteries were held inside.

Now, twelve full years later, we have all uncovered the countless mysteries that school has offered us: from comma splices to the quadratic equation to finding out that Dr. Weeks really doesn't have an electric paddle that plugs into the wall. Here we now stand, at the pinnacle of our high school career—the consummation of twelve years of hard work. I want you each to pause and remember all the struggles and triumphs that have brought you here: the time your team won in kickball, the time you stayed up all night working on that paper and somehow got an A, and the time all your friends were jealous because your lab partner was the cutest girl in school. Let us never forget these moments, for this has been a magical time for us—we were the last class ever to spend our freshman year in the unique atmosphere of Carver School and under the compelling leadership of Mr. Harry Grayson. Our senior year has given us State Championships in Cross Country, Golf and Tennis and strong showings in all other sports; these victories have combined with everything from DECA to Decathlon to make our years at Tupelo High School unforgettable. Never again will we live like this. So, before we plunge into the "real world," let us make sure that we hold tightly to these memories. For no matter how hard life may become in the future, you will always be third place in the science fair and that cute guy or girl in your English class will always be in his or her seat, waiting for you to get enough nerve to talk to him. Yes, this has truly been a magical time, but we could not have done it alone.

It has long been said that "Behind every good man is a great woman." Now, while some may question this theory, no one can deny that behind all of us students here tonight are hundreds of very hard working parents, grandparents, and guardians. Through their prompting, prodding, and sometimes pleading, they have pushed us to our fullest potential. They shared our defeats and our victories—they consoled us when we lost our lunch money, and they rejoiced with us when we passed our spelling test. Truly, our parents deserve more credit than we can ever give them, nevertheless I now ask all of the proud parents and guardians here tonight to stand and, classmates, please join me in applauding those who have brought us here tonight. (Applause.)

Our teachers are a group of people who deserve an equally immeasurable amount of credit. From the minute we stepped into elementary school, our teachers have shaped and molded us into thinking, feeling, and questioning human beings. They are special people who care enough about our futures to devote their lives to ensuring our success. Each day our teachers pursue the enormous task of preparing America's youth to become productive members of society. Although they receive little pay and often less recognition, our teachers continue to dedicate themselves to building and educating our youth. So I would like all teachers and administrators here tonight, from kindergarten to grade twelve, to please stand. Let's recognize our outstanding teachers and administrators. (Applause.)

The work of teachers, parents, and countless others has brought us here to this great threshold. Beyond lies a labyrinth of relationships, salaries, and W-2 Tax forms—of job interviews, car payments, and mothers-in-law. No one path leads through this maze of humanity. Each one of us must travel his own road to adulthood. Some of us will head directly into a workplace that is the backbone of today's society. Others will p[ur]sue further education in college or perhaps service in the United States Armed Forces. Whatever our plans may be, we all have one thing in common—tonight is the ceremonial end to our childhood. No longer will Mom or Dad be there to remind us of meetings or deadlines. No one will tell us when to wake up, how to dress, or when to come home at night. The freedoms and responsibilities of independence are ours. It is our obligation to make the best of them.

The American journalist Sydney J. Harris once said that "We have not passed that subtle line between childhood and adulthood until we move from the passive voice to the active voice—that is until we have stopped saying, 'It got lost,' and say, 'I lost it.'" No statement can more accurately describe the situation which we now face. We can no longer turn on the television, hear a report about the declining state of our country, and turn passively from the problem. This country belongs as much to us as it does to any adult here tonight. It is not "up to our parents" to decide which direction this country will take—it is up to us. And if we want to insure that our children will have all the opportunities that we have had, we must take an active role in our country's government now by educating ourselves and voting. Freedom is a double-edged sword: its benefits are many, but its responsibilities are great.

We have no excuse for failure. There is an entire world full of opportunities out there. New frontiers are discovered almost daily that will improve our lives and provide thousands of jobs. Our responsibility is to seek these opportunities and to reap all the benefits they may offer. The quality of our lives—and this world—depends solely on our efforts.

So, tonight, as we say our final farewell to Tupelo High School and the leadership of Mr. Dale Dobbs and Dr. Mike Walters, I urge all of us to meet the world with chins high and chests out. We have come a long way in twelve years, but the vast majority of our lives still remains uncharted. There are many roads yet to be traveled, many questions yet to be answered. I charge us to venture boldly into the world, living every day of our lives by the creed of Tennyson's *Ulysses*: "To strive, to seek, to find, and not to yield"—and above all, to meet every new opportunity with the wide-eyed enthusiasm of that first grader in all of us.

EDDIE EAGLE GUN SAFETY PROGRAM[3]
Marion P. Hammer

President, National Rifle Association of America (NRA); registered lobbyist since 1976; Executive Director of Unified Sportsmen of Florida since 1978; NRA certified firearm safety instructor; SCOPE Second Amendment Award, 1992.

Editors' introduction: On September 1, 1995, at the American Legion's 1995 annual convention, Ms. Marion P. Hammer, then Vice-President of the NRA, gave this keynote address in the Indianapolis Convention Center, Indiana. Referring to notes, she spoke to a combined assembly of 250 delegates from the American Legion National Commissions on Americanism, Education, and Children and Youth. Also attending were members of the American Legion Auxiliary and distinguished guests. The audience included Boys and Girls State gun safety award winners as well as adults. Hammer received the American Legion's 1995 National Education Award for the NRA's Eddie Eagle Gun Safety Program for Children. Prior to Hammer's speech, the delegates heard a presentation supporting a Constitutional Amendment to protect the American flag.

After the bombing at the Oklahoma City federal building, U.S. Senators considered legislation to "help Federal law-

[3]Delivered at the Indianapolis Convention Center, IN, on September 1, 1995, at 1:30 p.m.

enforcement officials deal with terrorist incidents"; however, the debate "bogged down over the . . . issue of handguns" (Jerry Gray, *New York Times*, June 7, 1995). Later, Bob Barr, "new point man for the NRA" in the U.S. House, and Chair of the Firearms Legislation Task Force, planned to have the ban on assault weapons repealed (Francis X. Clines, *New York Times*, Dec. 10, 1995). On March 22, 1996, the U.S. House passed the repeal 239 to 173. In his speech at Georgetown University, July 6, 1995, concerned about the level of violence in America, President Clinton maintained: "I don't have a problem with saying, look these assault weapons are primarily designed to kill people. . . . And I'm sorry if you don't have a new one that you can take out in the woods somewhere, to a shooting contest, but you'll get over it. Shoot with something else—(laughter and applause)—I'm glad you're clapping . . . but remember, the other people are good people who honestly believe what they say. That's the importance of this debate. . . . The NRA that I knew . . . for years were the people who did hunter education programs" (White House text).

Reporter Mike Williams (*Atlanta Journal/Atlanta Constitution* Dec. 22, 1995) described Hammer as "a 56-year-old chain-smoking, blunt-spoken grandmother who pushed through Florida's concealed weapons law, a model adopted by many other states, and who opposes the ban on assault weapons." She grew up on her grandparents farm after her father was killed on Okinawa in World War II. "Much of what I am today," Hammer recalled, "comes from the values and the hard work of growing up on that farm." Hammer explained to the editors of this anthology that her purpose in the address below was "to show the parallels of the origins, missions, and the work of the American Legion and National Rifle Association of America in the furtherance of Freedom, Liberty, and support for the safety and welfare of America's youth." To accomplish that goal, Hammer gave a "brief history of the two organizations and explanations of NRA's youth programs." One week later, the address was shown over National Empowerment Television, with the potential of reaching 7 million households. The speech was featured in American Legion's *The Dispatch* (Sept. 2, 1995), circulation, 20,000; aired September 9, 1995 at the NRA's National Board of Directors meeting in Virginia; printed in the *Congressional Record*; excerpted in *American Hunter* and *American Rifleman*, total circulation, 3.5 million; shown in *Reports from Washington*, a monthly video magazine, distribution 4,500; and printed in NRA's "Eagle Eye" news-letter, readership 3.5 million. The NRA has received numerous requests for videotapes of Hammer' s speech, for example, for an Albany, Oregon banquet. If she had the speech to do over again, Hammer "wouldn't change anything." Hammer was to become president of the NRA in 1996, but assumed that office early when Tom Washington, the 1995 president, died of a heart attack. Hammer is the first woman to be president of the NRA.

Marion P. Hammer's speech: The American Legion and the National Rifle Association of America are perhaps the two most dedicated, patriotic, country-flag-Constitution-and-freedom loving organizations in America.

And I am deeply honored to have an opportunity to stand before one of those organizations to represent the other.

Both organizations, founded in the bedrock of Liberty by military officers and enlisted men, dedicated themselves to principles of FREEDOM, PATRIOTISM and JUSTICE. Both organizations have become a part of the fiber and fabric of our nation's history.

The National Rifle Association of America, founded in November, 1871, has a distinguished history of education and training. Established to teach the skills of marksmanship and training to defend and protect our great nation and the Freedom provided by our Constitution, the NRA is the nation's leader in firearms safety and training.

And, the NRA is the sentry that stands watch over the Second Amendment—the amendment that guarantees our right to keep and bear arms and assures our ability to defend our nation and ourselves.

The American Legion, was conceived in March, 1919, at the Caucus in Paris, France by battle weary patriots waiting to return home from the physical battle to preserve Freedom in World War I. These brave men and women who had given so much of themselves to our nation, were destined to continue their sacrifice as they organized to preserve our nation's future in peace time as well as in battle.

The spirit and love of America beats strong in the hearts of our two great organizations that are committed to the future through the programs we provide for the youth of America. In 1918, the words of William Tyler Page were adopted by the United States House of Representatives as the "AMERICAN CREED." And within that creed are some very moving words. William Tyler Page wrote that this Nation was . . . : "[E]stablished upon the principles of freedom, equality, justice and humanity for which American patriots sacrificed their lives and fortunes. I therefore believe it is my duty to my country to love it, to support its Constitution, to obey its laws, to respect its flag, and to defend it against all enemies. . . . " DEFEND IT AGAINST ALL ENEMIES. Strong words with deep meaning.

Since our forefathers carved America out of the wilderness, our nation has faced many enemies. American patriots for generations, have made many sacrifices for freedom.

In 1945, in enemy action at Okinawa, my father added his name to the long roll call of American patriots who have paid the ultimate price—who have given their lives to the cause of freedom. The roll call is long, the sacrifices are many, and those of us who breathe freedom's air today, owe them. And we owe the men and women who came home bearing the scars of battle. We have a duty to continue in their footsteps. We owe it to them to carry America's flag against our enemies until we can hand it over to the next generation.

Today, America has new enemies. Enemies that are tearing at the fabric of our heritage and our society. Those enemies are moral decay, disrespect, parental neglect, dependence on government, and phony quick-fix government solutions to complex social problems.

America's children are the victims of those enemies. Because we love our country, our flag, our Constitution and our Freedom, we have a duty to America's youngsters. They are the future of America. We must love and nurture them. We must teach them values and strengths. Teach them discipline, self-reliance, respect and honor. Teach them to love America and what it stands for.

Through your youth programs and our youth programs, we are making a difference. And working together with other community groups, we can make an even bigger difference.

The NRA's Eddie Eagle Gun Safety program for young children is about much more than just teaching safety.

Youngsters learn safety but they also learn respect for guns and at the same time they learn respect for themselves when they gain knowledge.

They learn to resist temptation and not to touch a gun left carelessly unattended—that's discipline.

They learn to leave the area and make their friends and playmates leave the area—that's leadership.

They learn to quickly find and inform an adult of an unsafe situation—that's responsibility.

And when an adult has removed the gun and the area is safe again, they learn pride and a sense of accomplishment and self-worth for having used their knowledge and skills.

In our youth marksmanship programs and youth hunting programs, they learn values other than how to shoot safely and accurately. They learn concentration, commitment, sportsmanship, self-reliance, teamwork, citizenship, and conservation of our natural resources—values that are just as important as skills.

I am a mother and a grandmother and I know that when NRA reaches out and takes the hand of a child, we are touching America's future.

I know that when you love a child and give your time and patience to teaching values, patriotism, and skills, you are investing in the future.

I know that when you win the heart of a child and enrich his or her life with knowledge, you are building a solid foundation for the next generation.

I know that within the body of this nation, the hearts of many children long for someone to reach out to them with kindness, knowledge and guidance.

The NRA is committed to expanding our programs, to reaching out to more children and to investing in the future by helping to instill values and to build character in the youngsters we touch throughout America.

Today, you have honored the National Rifle Association of America for its Eddie Eagle Gun Safety Program and I am privileged to be here to accept your award.

And I am proud to tell you that this program has now been taught to over 7 million youngsters—7 million youngsters whom we hope will be the safest generation our nation has ever seen.

On behalf of the NRA, I thank you sincerely for this honor, and I promise you that I am committed to doing everything that I can to help the NRA continue its mission of teaching America's youth the fundamentals of what made our nation great.

If we all work together to fulfill our duty to our country and to the dedicated men and women who have given so much to keep us free, our children and our grandchildren and generations to follow them will learn to love their freedom, their country, their flag, their Constitution and THEMSELVES.

Thank you—each and every one of you—for the sacrifices you have made for our country. God bless you all, and God bless America.

THE IMAGINATION OF PREPARED MINDS[4]
Neil L. Rudenstine

President, Harvard University; born, Ossining, NY, 1935; B.A., Princeton University, 1956; B.A., 1959 and M.A., 1960 Oxford University; Ph.D., Harvard University, 1964; professor and administrator, Princeton University, 1968–88; Executive Vice President, Andrew W. Mellon Foundation, 1988–91; Fellow of the American Academy of Arts and Sciences.

Editors' introduction: Harvard University held its 344th commencement on June 8, 1995. As part of the week's activities, there were symposia on Vietnam, women's health issues, the criminal justice system, and international development. On the 6th, the Phi Beta Kappa Literary Exercises sponsored Orator Margaret Geller and Poet John Hollander. Under a tent in the rain in front of Harvard's Tercentenary Theater, Harvard Yard, Cambridge, MA, Dr. Neil L. Rudenstine, President of Harvard, spoke to approximately 20,000 Harvard alumni, faculty, administrators, graduating students, and their families. The address was preceded by morning commencement exercises and the conferring of degrees and honorary degrees. One student spoke in Latin. Hank Aaron, 61, baseball's homerun king, asked students to support "affirmative action programs now under wide attack" by a Republican majority in Congress (Fox Butterfield, *New York Times*, June 9, 1995). Václav Havel, President of the Czech Republic, also addressed the crowd. As was true at many institutions, during the academic year Harvard had experienced its share of violence, suicide, and anxiety. Due to exhaustion, Rudenstine

---

[4]Delivered at Harvard University, Cambridge, MA, June 8, 1995, at 3:00 p.m.

had taken a leave of absence, reporting that he had "received 1,
500 letters from students declaring themselves equally burnt-out"
(Jonathan Freedland, *Guardian*, June 10, 1995). WGBX-TV, Boston, and WHRB-FM, Cambridge, broadcast Rudenstine's speech
and *The American Journal of Physics* (Oct. 1995) published the text.
In his address, Rudenstine reminded citizens and leaders that
"significant new knowledge depends on the rigorous work and
imagination of prepared minds."

Neil L. Rudenstine's speech: Fifty years ago, as World War II
was coming to an end, Harvard graduates and their families gathered in this Yard for Commencement. The occasion was the same
as today. But the mood was very different. Victory had been declared in Europe, but we were still at war in the Pacific. The Commencement audience was much smaller than usual, and so the
gathering was held not here, in this space, but in the Sever Quad-
rangle, off to my left. President Conant explained that more than
25,000 Harvard graduates and students were still in uniform.
The Harvard Commencement of 1945, he told the audience, was
a purely local gathering because of national restrictions on war-
time travel. The usual daylong activities of Commencement were
condensed into two hours.

And yet the day—while in some ways solemn—was essentially
one of affirmation and hope. One of the honorary degree recipients—and the principal speaker—was Sir Alexander Fleming,
the renowned British bacteriologist. It was Fleming, in 1928, who
had discovered penicillin. And it was penicillin that had saved
thousands and thousands of lives during the war: a war in which
so many Harvard students, faculty, and alumni served with great
courage and distinction—and in which so many gave their lives.

But on Commencement Day fifty years ago, Fleming did not
speak about conflict and destruction. He spoke instead about the
importance to society of scientific discovery. He talked in an unas-
suming and personal way about the role of chance—of serendipi-
ty—in research, as well as in his own life.

As a young man, Fleming had spent five years as a shipping
clerk. He couldn't afford the medical education he wanted. Then
fortune intervened: a relative left him a legacy that was enough
to launch him in his medical studies. He earned his degree, served
in World War I, and went on to a career in biological research,
studying bacteria.

Within a decade, fortune intervened again, this time as Fleming was working in his laboratory. "I did not ask for a spore of *penicillium notatum* to drop on my culture [plate]," he said. "[And] when I saw certain changes [take place there], I had not the slightest suspicion that I was at the beginning of something extraordinary. . . . That same mould [spore] might have dropped on [any one] of my [other] culture plates, and there would have been no visible change to direct [my] special attention to it. . . . However, somehow or other, everything [fit] in. . . . There was an appearance which called for investigation—with the result that now, after various ups and downs, we have penicillin."

Why did Fleming tell this story on that particular Harvard Commencement day? He said he wanted to offer some advice to young researchers in pursuit of new knowledge. "Never," he said, "never neglect an extraordinary appearance or happening. It may be a false alarm and lead to nothing. But it may, on the other hand, be the clue provided by fate to lead you to some important advance."

We can now see, from our own vantage point, that there was also another significance to Fleming's remarks: he was already helping to shift our focus from the war that was ending, to the peace that was about to begin. His own personal experience reminded everyone that research and discovery could lead to dramatic and unpredictable advances by society, and by all individuals.

In fact, as we know, our own nation began to invest heavily in basic and applied research during the war years, and increased that investment afterward. Our major universities were seen as senior partners in this enterprise—and not only in research, but in the training of graduate and professional students in many different fields. We need to remember (and it can hardly be stressed enough) that advanced education—providing the constant stream of physicians and health professionals, educators, architects, business leaders, religious leaders, lawyers, government officials and other public servants—such advanced education depends most of all on a creative faculty engaged in significant research and discovery at major universities.

Without such a faculty, and without support for its research, neither Harvard nor any other university can carry out its fundamental mission, or achieve its own goals and those of society. Research and advanced education are inescapably linked to one another. Neither can flourish without the other.

I want to stress this point today because we have reached what may be a critical turning point in our nation's commitment to the creation of important new knowledge and understanding. Decisions now being made in Washington will have a profound effect on the future of research and education in this country. The stakes are very high. And the issue is not receiving the urgent and widespread attention it deserves—because this is certainly the most hazardous moment with respect to federal support for higher education in this country during the postwar period.

In the fifty years since Alexander Fleming spoke at Harvard—it is no exaggeration to say—basic research at universities has done much to transform our world.

• We should remember, for example, the discovery of the structure of DNA—in 1953—which has increased our understanding of almost every aspect of our biological nature, which began the revolution in genetics, and which led to the creation of the entire new industry of biotechnology.
• We should consider the computer revolution—the ways in which it has changed how we learn, how we transmit and access information, how we solve problems that were previously insoluble.
• Think about microwaves, plastics, optical fibers, laser discs, superconductors, weather and communications satellites, and many other devices and new materials that have become so much a part of our daily lives that we hardly even notice them any more.
• Or the advances in understanding cancer, heart disease, and other illnesses including mental illnesses. Think how much has been accomplished, but how much more work there is still to be done.

How we travel, how we communicate, what we eat, what we do with our free time, how we protect our environment, how we make a living—all these aspects of our lives have increasingly come to depend in essential ways on the discoveries that flow from our basic and applied research.

The driving force behind this steady advance—as I suggested—has been the cooperation, for a full half-century and more, between our universities and the federal government. This joint enterprise has been based on a simple premise that was spelled out in a famous report whose fiftieth anniversary we are also marking this year. The report was titled *Science: The Endless*

Frontier. Its author was Vannevar Bush—who also received a Harvard honorary degree, in 1941, when he was the principal speaker at our Commencement.

"Progress in the war against disease depends upon a flow of new scientific knowledge," Bush wrote in 1945. "New products new industries, and more jobs require continuous additions to knowledge . . . and the application of that knowledge to practical purposes. Science . . . provides no panacea for individual, social, and economic ills," he continued. But "without scientific progress, no amount of achievement in other directions can insure our health, prosperity, and security as a nation in the modern world."

These words are no less true today than fifty years ago. But our national mood, and certainly our sense of perspective, have changed. Today, we are more skeptical about institutions and what they can achieve. As a society, we have much less patience for long-term investments and long-range solutions. In fact, we have less patience for many things that require it. It is true, in addition, that the financial resources at our disposal are more constrained, and we face difficult choices about how to spend these resources. In such a climate, basic research—which has no broad or obvious constituency in our national politics—finds itself very seriously at risk.

A scientist spends weeks, months, even years studying the genetic make-up of baker's yeast. It sounds completely irrelevant, and might at first seem to be an easy target for ridicule. Later, we find out that the results of this work can help pave the way for a breakthrough in understanding the basis of colon cancer.

A team of physicists studies how protons shift energy levels inside the nuclei of atoms—not something that most of us worry about very much in our daily lives. But years later, the work leads to magnetic resonance imaging—MRI—an astonishingly precise tool that allows us to picture and to study normal and abnormal structures inside the human body. With other imaging devices, we can now watch parts of the brain and other organs in action; and we can begin to diagnose many diseases in ways that we could hardly have imagined before.

This is only the smallest handful of possible examples, illustrating what has been accomplished in the last half-century— thanks to our national conviction that discovery and increased understanding will constantly lead to real and tangible benefits, of many kinds, for all of us. Now, at a time when our ability to solve increasingly complicated problems—in the economy, in international affairs, in health, in ethnic relations, in technology—depends so much on intelligent leadership; on people who can both analyze and act; on research that can illuminate patterns in behavior, or the deepest puzzles in nature: at such a time we cannot afford to give up on the basic commitments and investments that have been so much a source of our collective human and economic strength.

The question many people are asking today is whether we can *afford* to make such investments in research and education. This is now—and always—an essential question to keep before us. But the other question we must ask—as we look to the future of our society as a whole—is whether we can afford *not* to make such investments.

We dare not underestimate the dangers—even if they are not immediately apparent. If, for instance, the enterprise of basic science is seriously damaged at the National Institutes of Health, the National Science Foundation, and other agencies, we may not see or feel the most profound effects either today or tomorrow. After all, it has taken fully forty years since the discovery of the structure of DNA to begin to realize what it will finally yield in terms of medical, social, and economic benefits. So we may well persuade ourselves into thinking that today's budget cuts will really have no profound impact. But that would be a very great mistake. The total impact will be felt later—in a decade, or even two. And then, it will be too late to turn back the clock—and it will cost a very great deal more to rebuild something that now needs only to be kept in good repair.

Many people in the Congress and the Executive Branch understand this. Many have been working hard, helping to follow the thoughtful, careful approach that is needed—and they have done so courageously, and with some real effect. The effort is bipartisan, and continuous. But our many leaders in Congress need to know that all the rest of us care, and that we too want to help. They cannot, in the current national climate, manage this entire formidable job on their own.

With them, we should remember another of Alexander Fleming's remarks fifty years ago. "The unprepared mind," he said, "cannot see the outstretched hand of opportunity." Curiosity alone does not produce new knowledge. Fortuity alone does not produce new knowledge. Rather, significant new knowledge depends on the rigorous work and imagination of *prepared* minds. It depends on excellent education. It depends on a climate of free inquiry, in which individuals have the flexibility and support that they need to follow their deepest insights and intuitions, in discovering new knowledge about human nature and the natural world.

In closing, let us remember, too, that Alexander Fleming almost did not make it to medical school. A small legacy from a relative happened to come his way. Without that financial help, we might well never have heard of Fleming—and we might never have had the benefit of his own well-prepared mind.

In the years since World War II—though we sometimes forget this fact—higher education in America has become far more accessible than ever before. Our society's conviction about the importance of educational opportunity—as expressed in our public policy and in the constant generosity of so many individuals—has steadily opened doors to women and men of talent and energy, from all backgrounds and walks of life, even when their financial means have been very modest. The commitment to provide financial aid to students in need—the commitment to openness and inclusiveness in our colleges and universities—has been one of the defining achievements of American society in the last fifty years.

For example, the Harvard class of 1945 included the first Harvard graduates who were supported by scholarships under the GI Bill of Rights—one of the great steps forward in expanding access to American higher education. In the following decades, we have seen even broader efforts to open the doors of our colleges and universities. Here, as in the case of scientific research, the key to progress has been a powerful partnership between educational institutions and the government—as well as generous private donors and, of course, our students and their families.

Here, too, we have arrived at a major crossroads. There are proposals on the table in Washington that would turn back the clock in significant ways. There are deeply troubling signs that an immensely productive investment in financial aid and access to education is in increasing danger.

For instance, the idea of beginning to charge interest on student loans from the moment a student enrolls in college would—

if adopted—add very substantially to student debt: for graduate students as well as for undergraduates. The proposals to freeze or cut campus-based aid programs such as work-study, or to freeze the Pell Grant program, are no less disturbing.

We must not let these and similar reversals take place. President Conant told us why, when he spoke here, fifty years ago. Broad access to education, he said, "is the great instrument created by American democracy to secure the foundations of a republic of free [people]." He remembered the many Harvard alumni who had given their lives to secure that freedom. And he pledged that we would honor their sacrifice—that we would work even harder, in times of peace, to serve society by continuing to advance knowledge, and by keeping the doors of educational opportunity open to everyone.

We must not, at this important moment, turn our backs on that pledge—for *all* of our sakes, and for the health of the nation. We have made good on our shared commitment to education, year after year, decade after decade, for these past fifty years. Let us not begin to falter now.

Honored guests, graduates, family, friends—I would now like to ask you all to rise. I ask that you join me in paying tribute to the Harvard men and women who gave so much of themselves—and especially the many who gave their lives—in the cause of freedom during the Second World War, and in later wars. I ask that you join me in honoring the Class of 1945, celebrating its 50th reunion today; and the Class of 1970, celebrating its 25th reunion. Let us celebrate the spirit of freedom that they did so much to protect and defend—and that *we* must protect and defend. We shall honor them, in the traditional way, by observing a moment of silence as the bell of Memorial Church tolls—in memory, and in thanks.

CUMULATIVE SPEAKER INDEX

1990-1996

A cumulative author index to the volumes of *Representative American Speeches* for the years 1937-1938 through 1959-1960 appears in the 1959-1960 volume, for the years 1960-1961 through 1969-1970 in the 1969-1970 volume, for the years 1970-1971 through 1979-1980 in the 1979-1980 volume, and for the years 1980-1981 through 1989-1990 in the 1989-1990 volume.

INDEX TO VOLUME 68 (1996)
BY SUBJECT

AFFIRMATIVE ACTION

AGED

Medical care

Under UCLA's elaborate system race makes a big difference. C. Shea. *The Chronicle of Higher Education* Ap. 28, 95. **68:3**

Racism has its privileges. R. W. Wilkins. *Nation* Mr. 27, '95. **68:3**

Crime

Violence, genes, and prejudice. J. Williams. *Discover* N. '94. **68:5**

Social conditions

The crisis of public order. A. Walinsky. *Atlantic Monthly* Jl. '95. **68:5**

BREGGIN, PETER ROGER, 1936–

About

The biology of violence. R. Wright. *New Yorker* Mr. 13, '95. **68:5**

BUCHANAN, PATRICK

Republican candidate for president. *Vital Speeches of the Day* My. 15, '95. **68:1**

About

A potent trinity—God, country & me. D. Corn. *Nation* Je. 26, '95. **68:1**

Fair trade, foul politics. R. Ponnuru. *Nationl Review* N. 6, '95. **68:4**

BUDGET

Balanced budgets and unreasonable expectations. *Challenge* S. '95. **68:2**

Balancing the federal budget. *Congressional Digest* F. '95. **68:2**

Economic impact of a balanced budget. *Congressional Digest* F. '95. **68:2**

Unbalancing the economy. *Nation* Mr. 13, '95. **68:2**

Why the deficit? L. Bentsen. *The Wall Street Journal* N. 3, '94. **68:2**

Facing the painful truth: the 1995 budget debate. R. J. Bresler. *USA Today* Jl. '95. **68:2**

Off balance. R. Eisner. *N.Y. Times* Mr. 19, '94. **68:2**

Trimming the trillions. R. T. Gray. *Nation's Business* Je. '95. **68:2**

Reversing the tide. D. Hage and others. *U.S. News & World Report* Ap. 3, '95. **68:2**

How to balance the budget—for real. F. Lalli. *Money* Ja. '95. **68:2**

Guts check. C. Lochhead. *Reason* Jl. '95. **68:2**

How to shrink the U.S. budget deficit. G. Marotta. *Vital Speeches of the Day* O. 15, '95. **68:2**

Budget-balancing GOP senators get an edge. J. McTague. *Barron's* My. 8, '95. **68:2**

No courage to cut. J. M. Wall. *The Christian Century* Ja. 25, '95. **68:2**

A budget train wreck? K. T. Walsh. *U.S. News & World Report* Ag. 28-S 4, '95. **68:2**

Attention, deficit disorder. J. Weisberg. *New York* Ja. 2, '95. **68:2**

CLINTON, WILLIAM JEFFERSON, 1946–
Commercial policy

Relations with Congress

COMMUNITY NOTIFICATION LAWS

COMMUNITY SERVICE

COMPUTER CRIMES

CONGRESS
United States

CONSTITUTION
United States
Amendments

COST EFFECTIVENESS

EDUCATION

Under UCLA's elaborate system race makes a big difference. C. Shea. *The Chronicle of Higher Education* Ap. 28, 95. **68:3**

Among white males, jokes, and anecdotes. R. Wilson. *The Chronicle of Higher Education* Ap. 28, 95. **68:3**

Continuing

The values of unions. A. J. Brindley. Speech delivered Ap. 6, '95. **68:6**

Benefits and responsibilities. B. Rogers. Speech delivered My. 24, '95. **68:6**

The imagination of prepared minds. N. L. Rudenstine. Speech delivered Je. 8, '95. **68:6**

ECONOMIC CONDITIONS

The threat of modernization. P. M. Kennedy. *New Perspectives Quarterly* Wint. '95. **68:4**

ECONOMIC DEVELOPMENT

Economic "miracles." D. R. Henderson. *Society* S/O. '95. **68:4**

Back to the future. F. Zakaria. *National Review* D. 11, '95. **68:4**

ECONOMIC HISTORY

Economic "miracles." D. R. Henderson. *Society* S/O. '95. **68:4**

ECONOMIC POLICY

Economic "miracles." D. R. Henderson. *Society* S/O. '95. **68:4**

Off balance. R. Eisner. *N.Y. Times* Mr. 19, '94. **68:2**

ENTITLEMENT SPENDING

Social security: sacred cow of entitlement programs. W. Hogeboom. *USA Today* N. '95. **68:2**

To cut or not to cut. R. Hoopes. *Modern Maturity* N. '94. **68:2**

Facing the painful truth: the 1995 budget debate. *USA Today* Jl. '95. **68:2**

Guts check. C. Lochhead. *Reason* Jl. '95. **68:2**

Entitlement reform: A key to america's economic future. P. G. Peterson. *Vital Speeches of the Day* F. 15, '95. **68:2**

EUGENICS

Closets full of bones. P. Quinn. *America* F. 18, '95. **68:1**

EX-CONVICTS

Thy neighbor's rap sheet. T. Carlson. *Policy Review* Spr. '95. **68:5**

FAMILY

The real root cause of violent crime. P. Fagan. *Vital Speeches of the Day* D. 15, '95. **68:5**

FEDERAL RESERVE BANK OF ATLANTA

About

The challenges and opportunities of the global marketplace. R. P. Forrestal. *Vital Speeches of the Day* S. 1, '95. **68:4**

Fair trade, foul politics. R. Ponnuru. *Nationl Review* N. 6, '95. **68:4**

A budget train wreck? K. T. Walsh. *U.S. News & World Report* Ag. 28-S 4, '95. **68:2**

SCHOOL VIOLENCE
Standing up to violence. R. C. Sautter. *Phi Delta Kappan* Ja. '95. **68:5**

SELF DEFENSE
A call to arms. R. Dillon. *Los Angeles* Ap. '94. **68:5**

SILVA RESERVOIR (MEXICO)
NAFTA's first real test. T. Nauman. *Audubon* S/O. '95. **68:4**

SMUGGLING
China's human traffickers. P. Kwong. *Nation* O. 17, '94. **68:1**

The new slave trade. M. Liu. *Newsweek* Je. 21, '93. **68:1**

SOCIAL SECURITY
Behind the numbers. A. Brinkley. *Modern Maturity* Jl/Ag. '95. **68:1**

Social security: sacred cow of entitlement programs. W. Hogeboom. *USA Today* N. '95. **68:2**

SOCIOLOGY
The biology of violence. R. Wright. *New Yorker* Mr. 13, '95. **68:5**

SOUTHEASTERN STATES
Economic conditions
The challenges and opportunities of the global marketplace. R. P. Forrestal. *Vital Speeches of the Day* S. 1, '95. **68:4**

SPECULATION
Dutch tulips and emerging markets. P. R. Krugman. *Foreign Affairs* Jl/Ag. '95. **68:4**

SQUATTER SETTLEMENTS
Mexico
Mexico and its discontents. D. W. Payne. *Harper's* Ap. '95. **68:1**

STRANGERS
The crisis of public order. A. Walinsky. *Atlantic Monthly* Jl. '95. **68:5**

TARIFFS
China
In a move to open its markets, China pledges to cut tariffs. A. Pollack. *N.Y. Times* N. 20, '95. **68:4**
United States
Fair trade, foul politics. R. Ponnuru. *Nationl Review* N. 6, '95. **68:4**

TEACHERS
Dismissals
Is affirmative action doomed? J. Rosen. *New Republic* O. 17, '94. **68:3**

WATER POLLUTION

Mexico

NAFTA's first real test. T. Nauman. *Audubon* S/O. '95. **68:4**

WHITE MEN

Employment

Planet of the white guys. B. Ehreneich. *Time* Mr. 13, '95. **68:3**

WOMEN

Observations and opportunities in the 90's. C. Black. Speech delivered Je. 20, '95. **68:6**

When communities flourish. H. R. Clinton. Speech delivered S. 5, '95. **68:6**

Country day values. R. E. Marier. Speech delivered Ag. 23, '95. **68:6**

Employment

Is affirmative action doomed? J. Rosen. *New Republic* O. 17, '94. **68:3**

WORLD TRADE ORGANIZATION (WTO)

Is America abandoning multilateral trade? J. E. Garten. *Foreign Affairs* N/D. '95. **68:4**

Fron GATT to WTO: the institutionlization of world trade. S. S. Pitroda. Ap. 1, '95. **68:4**

GOSHEN COLLEGE - GOOD LIBRARY

3 9310 01004678 5